Colin McEvedy **The Penguin Atlas of Recent History: Europe since 1815**

Maps devised by the author
and drawn by David Woodroffe

Penguin Books

INTRODUCTION

This *Atlas* is the concluding volume in a set of four which have as their theme the differentiation and evolution of European society. The first two volumes covered the Near East as well as Europe – all of it in the case of the volume on the Ancient World, about half in the *Medieval Atlas* – because European society was originally only part of a larger unit extending east as far as Iran: not till the late medieval period did the rift between Europe and south-west Asia widen beyond healing. And in the early modern volume, though the focus narrowed down to continental Europe, it was necessary to interrupt the main sequence of maps at intervals so as to show what was happening in the wider world: the pecking order in Europe was considerably influenced by the success or failure of overseas adventures. Now we can confine our attention, and our base map, to Europe alone.

Two cavils immediately present themselves: surely it was Victorian Britain's overseas empire that made her a great power? And, haven't the Americans played a critical role in European history ever since 1917? The answer to the first is a clear No. Britain was a great power in the nineteenth century because of the demographic and industrial upsurge that made her, on her home resources alone, the equal of any European nation; the Empire was an ornament that neither added to nor detracted from her essential stature. The answer to the second must be Yes, but the appearance of a *deus ex machina* doesn't alter the nature of the stage. Insofar as local history has any validity in the twentieth century, Europe remains a logical subject of study; anyhow, most of the players, even in the Second World War, were Europeans born and bred. Still, it is true that something is lacking in the post-war years, which is perhaps why I have skimped in this area. The defeat and dismemberment of Germany has meant that no purely European nation (a definition that excludes the USSR) can ever count as a superpower. We are out of the big league and don't need maps the way we used to.

A word about the lettering on the maps. The basic idea is that sovereign states have their names in capitals and that all other names, whether of peoples or places, are in lower case. Possession by a sovereign power is indicated by an upper-case label in brackets: e.g. Algeria (FRENCH). Up till 1918 the sovereign states are also given full political titles: e.g. K. OF FRANCE, FRENCH REPUBLIC, FRENCH EMPIRE; after 1918, when this sort of thing has lost most of its significance, the description is simplified to FRANCE. A minor refinement is that in the pre-1918 period simple descriptions indicate incomplete sovereignty: e.g. SERBIA was autonomous but still under Turkish suzerainty until 1878; it then became fully sovereign and so appears as P. OF SERBIA (after 1881, K. OF SERBIA).

The convention in the case of population maps is slightly different. Sovereign states are in upper case, their constituent provinces – where shown at all – in lower case; hence the figures for the latter are summed in the former. But some politically dependent states are shown as independent demographic units: e.g. ALGERIA is always written in upper case and its population is not included in the total for FRANCE. The conventions on the conurbation maps are explained in the keys; the only point to note here is that the labels apply to built-up areas, not local government units.

Putting this book together has given me great pleasure. It has been less fun for those in my immediate vicinity and this seems the moment to thank my wife Sarah for her forbearance, my secretary Sandra Cook for her diligence, and my friend Freddie Greenwell for his encouragement and advice. A house rule prevents me from thanking my publisher; this is a pity, because if there is 1 per cent of inspiration to the 99 per cent of perspiration, it derives from the imprint, which is not only a bird of noble lineage but a seal of good practice.

THE FRENCH REVOLUTION put Europe on the boil for twenty-five years. States and institutions that people had lived with for centuries vanished overnight; new ones with strange names appeared in their place. Every time there was a battle – and, particularly after Napoleon had become Emperor of the French, there were battles all the time – the whole political picture changed. What next year's alliances would be, what next year's map would look like, were questions no one could answer.

In 1815 all this stopped. Napoleon was packed off to St Helena and, at the Congress of Vienna, the representatives of the powers that had defeated him – the United Kingdom, Russia, Prussia and Austria – drew up a set of frontiers that were meant to last. And so they did. During the next thirty years there was only one change of importance, the break-up of the united Netherlands.

The Netherlands had been divided into northern and southern halves during the Protestant Reformation of the sixteenth century when the Calvinist Dutch in Holland cut themselves off from the Spanish-controlled, Catholic south. The southern half was inherited by the Austrians in the early eighteenth century, then, in 1793, conquered and annexed by the French. The Congress of Vienna was determined not to let the French get hold of it again and, as the Austrians weren't interested in resuming sovereignty, this partly French-speaking, entirely Catholic area was placed under the Dutch King, William of Orange. Unfortunately, King William and the clique of Dutch advisers who surrounded him couldn't resist the temptation to promote their language and religion in the south. This caused increasing discontent and in 1830 discontent became rebellion. King William's officers were ejected from Brussels, his initial attempt to reinstate them was frustrated and the rebels were able to proclaim the independence of the country, which, harking back

to Roman times when the area had been inhabited by the Celtic Belgae, they christened Belgium. Britain and France supported them, the other powers gave a grudging assent and by the end of the year Belgium was a kingdom in its own right.

Persuading King William of the wisdom of all this wasn't easy. Still determined to re-establish control, he invaded Belgium in force in 1831; it took a French army to stop him and a Franco-British blockade of the coast of Holland to make him agree to an armistice. Even then he wouldn't sign a formal peace treaty and didn't do so till 1838. His obstinacy brought him the return of much of Luxembourg (he got the part marked *L* on the map) and Limburg (the part marked *Lim*), both of which had been occupied by the Belgians in the interim.

The Franco-British understanding that made the birth of Belgium possible was a tribute to the liberal and common-sense attitudes of their governments. Elsewhere reaction reigned. The ruling cliques of the other three European powers – Prussia, Russia and Austria – were conservative in the extreme: they wanted no changes of any sort anywhere. In the specific instance of Belgium they reluctantly accepted an international guarantee of its frontiers as adequately containing the problem, but they made no secret of the fact that they would have preferred to have intervened on King William's side. It was only because Britain wouldn't countenance it that they had held back.

To a generation exhausted by revolutionary changes the conservative formulation had considerable appeal: after all, if everyone accepted that frontiers were immutable, there would be no more wars. But the aims of the 'Holy Alliance', as the understanding between Prussia, Russia and Austria was known, put it in automatic opposition to the nationalists that the Vienna settlement had incompletely satisfied (as in Germany), acknowledged in only a formal sense (as in Poland) or ignored completely (as in Italy). The arrangements made for

Germany were complicated and need extended presentation: this is given on pages 6–7. The Polish example is simple, for the Poles had wanted a country of their own but didn't get it: the 'Kingdom of Poland' set up by the Congress of Vienna was never more than a province of the Russian Empire and was officially reduced to this status after the unsuccessful uprising of 1830–31. Italian nationalism didn't even get this degree of recognition, the peninsula being divided into half a dozen principalities, all of which were, to a greater or lesser degree, Austrian satellites.[1]

Metternich, Austria's chief minister, would have denied there was any such thing as Italian nationalism anyway. 'Italy is a purely geographical expression' was one of his dicta. He had no scruple about shooting young hot-heads who raised the flag of United Italy – or of liberalism – anywhere in the peninsula, and no doubt that he was doing the right thing when he did: they were simply disturbers of the peace. In many ways he is the key figure of the era. He had represented Austria at the Congress of Vienna and had been in power ever since: the agreements he had reached then, he guarded still.

There was one part of Europe where no one, not even Metternich, could prevent change: the Balkans. Ottoman Turkey's grip on its European provinces was weakening year by year and the Christian peoples who formed the majority of the population there – Serbs, Romanians, Bulgars and Greeks – sensed that the hour of national liberation was near. The first to try their luck were the Serbs, who achieved autonomous status as early as 1817. Next were the Greeks, in 1821. Despite chaotic leadership, they too proved able to defeat the forces that the Sultan sent against them. Then they fell to fighting among themselves.

As it turned out, the Sultan hadn't given up Greece; he had simply turned the war over to Mohammed Ali, the Governor of Egypt. And Mohammed Ali's soldiers, trained and equipped on the European pattern, proved more effective than anything the Sultan had at his disposal. Indeed they made such short work of the rebels, first on Crete (1824) and then on the mainland (1825), that it seemed as if the Greek cause was doomed. But now it was the Greeks' turn to get outside aid, for, spurred on by emotions that had more to do with the glories of classical Hellas than the abject realities of the nineteenth-century Balkans, the Powers decided to intervene. The British, French and Russian Mediterranean fleets combined to sink the Turkish navy (in Navarino Bay in 1827), the Russians invaded the Balkans and Turkish Transcaucasia (1828), and the Sultan was forced to sign a treaty recognizing Greek independence (1829). By the same treaty (of Adrianople) he also conferred autonomy on the Romanian principalities of Moldavia and Wallachia and ceded the Danube delta (d) and various Transcaucasian towns to Russia.[2]

Further afield – and outside the area of our main interest – note the French occupation of Algeria (which evolved from a punitive expedition dispatched in 1830), the Ottoman Turks' control of Libya (resumed in 1835 after an interval of more than a century) and their loss of control over Egypt (effectively an independent state since the 1830s when Mohammed Ali and the Sultan had fallen out).

[1]. Two of them actually had Habsburg rulers (the Habsburgs being Austria's imperial family); as recently as 1847 it had been three, for Marie Louise, the Austrian Archduchess who had been Napoleon's second Empress, was given the Duchy of Parma as part of the Vienna settlement. When she died, the real Duke of Parma, who in the interim had been parked in the mini-Duchy of Lucca, got his Duchy back again, bar a few frontier towns, transferred by prior agreement to Modena; as part of the same deal Tuscany was allowed to absorb Lucca.

The state labelled Piedmont-Sardinia on the map has a confusing geography and nomenclature. It consisted of four elements: the Duchy of Savoy on the French side of the Alps (*Sav* on the map); the Principality of Piedmont on the Italian side (*Pied*); Liguria (*Lig*), the coastal strip that had once been the Republic of Genoa (and had only been added to Piedmont at the Congress of Vienna); and the island of Sardinia. The heart of the state was Piedmont and its capital was the Piedmontese city, Turin; however, Piedmont was only a principality whereas Sardinia was a kingdom, so contemporaries, taking the senior title, referred to the whole as Sardinia. Similarly, they called the Piedmontese soldiers and bureaucrats Sardinians even though the vast majority of them had never set eyes on the island. This usage doesn't look right nowadays and in the text I've opted for Piedmontese as the normal adjective.

[2]. The only other frontier changes in the period 1815–48 were the acquisition by Serbia of a strip of territory on its southern border (ratified by the Ottoman authorities in 1833) and Austria's annexation in 1846 of the Republic of Cracow. The Serbian gains were the result of Russian pressure on the Turks: being both Slav and Orthodox, the Serbs were regarded with special favour by the Russians. The Austrians' annexation of the theoretically free Polish city of Cracow was made with the agreement of the two other 'protecting powers', Russia and Prussia: it can be seen as a footnote to the late-eighteenth and early-nineteenth century treaties that partitioned Poland between the three of them.

Ceuta, Melilla and Heligoland
Ceuta and Melilla are two small towns on the Mediterranean coast of Morocco which have been held by Spain since 1580 and 1470 respectively. Their positions are marked (by stars) on this and all other relevant maps, but, as their status never changes, they are only named on this map and the last one.

Heligoland is a tiny island in the North Sea near the root of the Danish Peninsula. Taken by the British during the Napoleonic wars, it was held by them till 1890 when it was ceded to Germany in return for Zanzibar. Its position is marked by a square, as are the other isolated naval bases of the era, Gibraltar and Malta. However, whereas these two are important enough to be labelled every time they appear, Heligoland is not, so it is only named on this map and the map for 1910.

UNITED KINGDOM

K. OF SWEDEN AND NORWAY

RUSSIAN EMPIRE

K. OF DENMARK

Heligoland
(BRITISH)

the Netherlands

K. OF
HOLLAND

K.
OF   PRUSSIA

K. OF
BELGIUM

Lim

Poland

L

MINOR
GERMAN
STATES

Cracow

unsubdued
Circassians

K. OF FRANCE

AUSTRIAN EMPIRE

MOLDAVIA

SWISS

Sav

PARMA
MODENA

d

Pied

PIEDMONT-SARDINIA

WALLACHIA

Lig

TUSCANY

Lucca

SERBIA

K. OF
PORTUGAL

PAPAL
STATE

MONTENEGRO

OTTOMAN EMPIRE

K. OF SPAIN

K. OF THE
TWO SICILIES

Ionian
Islands
(BRITISH)

K. OF
GREECE

Gibraltar

BRITISH POSSESSIONS IN THE MEDITERRANEAN

Navarino

Ceuta
and Melilla
(SPANISH)

Algeria
(FRENCH)

K. OF MOROCCO

BEYLIK
OF TUNIS

Malta

Cretè

Libya

VICEROYALTY OF EGYPT

1 January
1848

THE CONGRESS OF VIENNA tidied up the map of Germany, reducing the number of states from the eighteenth-century total of about three hundred to thirty-eight. It also recognized the great upsurge of pan-German patriotism that had occurred during the final campaigns against Napoleon by creating a German Confederation, in which all thirty-eight were enrolled. Excluded were the Germans who lived in the Danish Duchy of Schleswig (1 on the map), the French provinces of Alsace and Lorraine (3) and Switzerland; otherwise the Confederation covered the entire German-speaking area. The voting was weighted towards the bigger states, but the non-German parts of the Austrian Empire and the Kingdom of Prussia did not count for this purpose; the Confederation boundary did, however, include the Austrian provinces of Bohemia (4), Moravia (5), and Carniola (6), despite the fact that all were predominantly Slav (Czech in the first two instances, Slovene in the third).

The only trouble with the Confederation as an instrument of unity was that the princes who ran it had no interest in making it work: better be a small prince than someone else's subject, was their view. So, between 1815 and 1848 the Confederation achieved exactly nothing. However, the impulse to unity was not entirely stifled; it surfaced in the *Zollverein*, the German Customs Union. Everyone could see that thirty-eight different customs barriers had to be bad for trade and, once the princes were persuaded that no loss of sovereignty was involved, the movement to create a single tariff wall for Germany made rapid progress: by 1848 the *Zollverein* included all the states of the Confederation bar Austria and a small bloc in the north-west.

The *Zollverein* was hardly enough to satisfy the nationalists, though: they constantly bemoaned the fragmentation of the Fatherland, comparing its plight with that of Italy. But, unlike the Italians, the Germans had no foreign tyrant to blame for their misfortunes. Or, to be exact, only one – and a very small one at that. In the extreme north the King of Denmark held, as he had done since the Middle Ages, the Duchies of Schleswig (90 per cent German) and Holstein (2 on the map and 100 per cent German). The pan-German patriots were determined that this situation should not continue a moment longer than necessary and in the ancient German laws of inheritance – which, unlike the Danish law, did not allow titles of this sort to pass through a female – they saw their opportunity. For by the beginning of 1848 King Christian of Denmark was visibly fading, while his only son Frederick was forty years old, had two dissolved marriages behind him and no children. There was a collateral line through which the throne of Denmark could pass, but this contained a female link, so the Duchies had to take a different route. Just as the connections between Hanover and the United Kingdom had been broken (to the relief of both sides) on the accession of Queen Victoria to the throne of Great Britain in 1837, so the link between Denmark and Schleswig-Holstein would break on Frederick's death.

Unfortunately the Danes, unlike the British, did not want to give up their German fiefs and they now announced a new constitution for the Duchies that – to no one's surprise – said inheritance in the female line was perfectly alright. As the Germans in the Duchies made it plain that they would secede immediately if any attempt was made to apply this constitution, a confrontation on the issue appeared inevitable.

On the main sequence of maps in this Atlas there isn't room to show more than the two largest of the German states, Austria and Prussia. The second of the two maps opposite attempts to remedy this deficiency; it shows by means of shadings the dominions of the five states in the next rank: the Kingdom of Bavaria (which, like its big brother Prussia, had received a detached Rhine province at the Congress of Vienna), the Kingdoms of Saxony, Hanover and Württemberg and the Grand Duchy of Baden. All of these had populations of more than a million. Also shown are the four free cities of the Confederation: Frankfurt, Lübeck, Bremen and Hamburg. Not shown are thirteen mini-states with populations of less than 100,000.

That leaves eleven middling-sized states with populations in the 100,000–750,000 range: Oldenburg, the two Mecklenburg duchies (Mecklenburg-Schwerin and Mecklenburg-Strelitz), Brunswick, the four Saxon duchies (Saxe-Weimar, Saxe-Coburg-Gotha, Saxe-Altenburg and Saxe-Meiningen), Hesse-Cassel (an electorate), Hesse-Darmstadt (a duchy) and the Duchy of Nassau. The map shows where these were to be found, but it doesn't attempt to delineate their convoluted frontiers.[1]

1. The Confederation membership had been reduced to thirty-seven in 1847 (thirty-three in the area of this map plus Austria, Prussia, Luxembourg and Holstein) by the amalgamation of two mini-principalities.

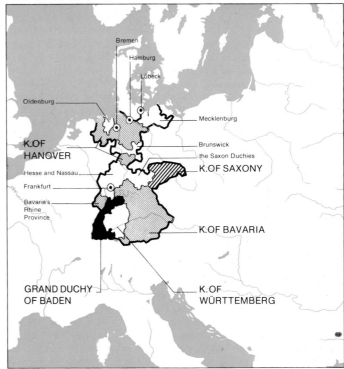

THE OVERALL PICTURE

1	Schleswig	4	Bohemia
2	Holstein	5	Moravia
3	Alsace-Lorraine	6	Carniola

Hanover and Oldenburg were to join the Customs Union in 1851–2.

THE MINOR STATES

Only five of these had populations of more than a million: Bavaria (4.4m), Saxony (1.9m), Hanover (1.8m), Württemberg (1.7m) and Baden (1.3m). The rest had about five millions between them.

GERMANY IN 1848

THE FIVE MAJOR POWERS of mid-nineteenth century Europe were, as you might expect, the ones with the biggest populations: Russia, France, Austria, the United Kingdom and Prussia. But population doesn't count for everything and they didn't rank in that order. Prussia, because it was more tightly knit, was stronger than Austria, and Britain, because of its industrial muscle, outranked both. Conversely, Spain, which had nearly as many people as Prussia (and as recently as 1815 had actually had more), didn't rate at all: it had fallen so far behind economically that it couldn't make its manpower effective.

Of the big five, four were nation states. It isn't difficult to define what one means by this: in each of these countries a majority of the citizenry shared a common language and religion. At least 90 per cent of Frenchmen spoke French and the same proportion belonged at least nominally to the Catholic Church. More than eight in every ten Prussians were German (the rest were mostly Poles) and of the Germans 70 per cent were Protestant. The Tsar's seventy million subjects included some notable minorities (five million Poles, three and a half million Finns, Ests, Letts and Latvians and three million assorted Caucasians), but that still left fifty millions who were both Russian and Orthodox. And the inhabitants of the British Isles were 90 per cent English-speaking and 70 per cent Protestant. Countries like these needed little holding together: they had an intrinsic cohesion. By contrast the Austrian Emperor ruled an ethnic mishmash that must have made him groan every time he thought about it. He and eight million of his subjects were German, but twice as many were Slavs of one sort or another (Czechs, Slovaks, Poles, Ruthenians, Slovenes, Croats and Serbs), five million were Hungarians, five million Italians and two million Romanians. What sort of a nation did that make?

The answer is none at all. The Austrian Empire was simply an accumulation of lands and peoples inherited or otherwise acquired by the Habsburg family over the centuries. The Congress of Vienna had done one of its tidying-up operations on it, so that it now formed a solid block of territory without outliers (such as the southern Netherlands had been in the eighteenth century); however, no one could do anything about the lack of racial coherence. Demands for autonomy, even for outright independence, were already being voiced by the Italians, Hungarians and Poles; one day the Czechs, Slovaks, Slovenes and Croats were bound to follow suit. No wonder the Emperor, on being told that one of his subjects was a good patriot, said irritably, 'Yes, but is he a patriot for me?'

One ethnic group did give the Emperor the sort of loyalty he was looking for, the Germans of his Austrian homeland. And in return he cherished them. They manned the bureaucracy, officered the army and generally reaped the benefits of the Empire. Maybe it was a bit of an old-fashioned concern, but such as it was, it was all theirs: every year that it stayed in business was a good year for them. Hence the ultra-conservative stance of Austrian politicians: other people might possibly benefit by change; they could only lose.

Behind its static political façade Europe was, in fact, experiencing revolutionary changes: the processes of urbanization and industrialization, considered overleaf, are two of the most important. A third is purely quantitative: there were quite simply more people, multiplying at a faster rate, than ever before. Since the beginning of the century numbers had risen by 50 per cent (Britain and Russia, the leaders in this race, notched up gains of 75 per cent, France, the laggard, a bare 25 per cent). And, as the half-century approached, the rate of increase was, if anything, accelerating.

Educated opinion regarded this as a bad thing. Thomas Malthus was the recognized expert on such matters and he had taught that, population increase being a geometric function and agricultural output an arithmetic one, more people meant less food per person and ultimately starvation. He couldn't have picked a better case to prove his point than Ireland. By 1845 population increase there had turned a mildly prosperous agricultural country into an unhappy land where every winter a quarter of the people starved. That year disaster struck when the potato crop, the staple of the poor, was destroyed by a fungal blight. Worse still, the same thing happened the next year. Those who could fled to England or the United States; of those who couldn't, nearly a million died. Ireland's population figures began to fall as fast as they had risen.

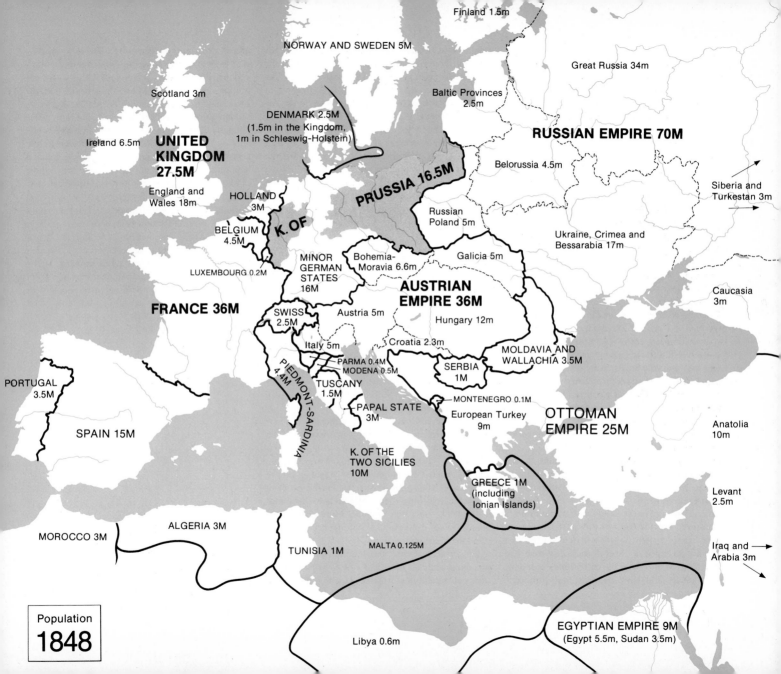

Finland 1.5m

NORWAY AND SWEDEN 5M

Great Russia 34m

Scotland 3m

DENMARK 2.5M
(1.5m in the Kingdom,
1m in Schleswig-Holstein)

Baltic Provinces
2.5m

RUSSIAN EMPIRE 70M

Ireland 6.5m

UNITED
KINGDOM
27.5M

PRUSSIA 16.5M

Belorussia 4.5m

England and
Wales 18m

HOLLAND
3M

Russian
Poland 5m

Siberia and
Turkestan 3m

K. OF

BELGIUM
4.5M

Galicia 5m

Ukraine, Crimea and
Bessarabia 17m

LUXEMBOURG 0.2M

MINOR
GERMAN
STATES
16M

Bohemia-
Moravia 6.6m

AUSTRIAN
EMPIRE 36M

Caucasia
3m

FRANCE 36M

SWISS
2.5M

Austria 5m

Hungary 12m

PORTUGAL
3.5M

Italy 5m

Croatia 2.3m

PIEDMONT-SARDINIA
4.4M

PARMA 0.4M
MODENA 0.5M
TUSCANY
1.5M

MOLDAVIA AND
WALLACHIA 3.5M

SERBIA
1M

SPAIN 15M

PAPAL STATE
3M

MONTENEGRO 0.1M

European Turkey
9m

OTTOMAN
EMPIRE 25M

Anatolia
10m

K. OF THE
TWO SICILIES
10M

GREECE 1M
(including
Ionian Islands)

Levant
2.5m

MOROCCO 3M

ALGERIA 3M

TUNISIA 1M

MALTA 0.125M

Iraq and
Arabia 3m

Population
1848

Libya 0.6m

EGYPTIAN EMPIRE 9M
(Egypt 5.5m, Sudan 3.5m)

EUROPE'S POPULATION in 1848 was not only larger than ever before; it was also more urban. There were more big towns than there had been a half-century earlier (forty-five with populations over 100,000 as against twenty-eight in 1800) and the biggest had grown to unheard-of sizes (London, which had been the only one on the million mark in 1800, was now well on the way to its third million). Moreover, in Britain, a new type of urban unit had appeared, the industrial conurbation. These grim cities – Manchester, Birmingham, Liverpool, Glasgow and Leeds are the ones to qualify for a place on this map – show how far Britain had moved from the country village, county town and capital city hierarchy that still characterized the rest of Europe.

The economic primacy these conurbations conferred on Great Britain is emphasized by every index of production. The United Kingdom was producing more than three-quarters of Europe's coal and well over half its iron. British engineers had developed two revolutionary forms of transport, the railway locomotive and the steamship, and British factories and yards built the best and the most of both. The capacity of the British textile industry was twice that of continental Europe's. Of course, things couldn't go on like this forever: as the rising British politician, Disraeli, warned parliament, 'The Continent will not suffer England to be the workshop of the world.' But for the time being it had to.

Besides being the first industrial nation, Britain stood out from the other European states because it was, at least for those who owned a modicum of property, a democracy. One in every eight Englishmen had the vote in the early nineteenth century, a proportion that the Reform Bill of 1832 raised to one in five.[1] To many outsiders it seemed likely that Britain's exceptionally liberal political system had something to do with its exceptional economic performance, and the argument that prosperity could be achieved through reform was often advanced by those who wanted to liberalize the autocratic regimes of the continental powers. This movement was particularly strong in France where the clock had been put back ridiculously far by the restored monarchy: only one in 300 Frenchmen had the vote in the 1820s, and that for a parliament that had hardly any powers at all. In 1830 the French refused to put up with this system any longer: the illiberal King Charles X was chased out of the country and his cousin, Louis-Philippe the 'Citizen King', put on the throne in his place. Louis-Philippe sanctioned a tenfold increase in the electorate and promised to rule like a British constitutional monarch.

The success of the liberals in France was an important factor in the Belgian rising which took place four weeks later. This may have been primarily anti-Dutch in its inspiration, but Belgian sentiment was also against anyone ruling as autocratically as William of Orange had; consequently, the first king of the Belgians found himself with a British-style parliament elected on a one-in-fifteen franchise. The benign attitude the British adopted towards Louis-Philippe and the new Belgian state was largely due to the way both copied British institutions: it was, after all, a guarantee of peaceable intent as well as a very acceptable form of flattery.

Not that everything was right in Britain. The new wealth being created there was distributed so unequally that rich and poor were – the phrase is another of Disraeli's – becoming Two Nations. Radical politicians didn't see a widening of the franchise as having much relevance for this problem and some, following continental thinkers, favoured a 'socialist' solution, which meant legislation guaranteeing everyone a job and a minimum standard of living.

In a world where many countries were imprisoning liberals, the chances of socialists getting their policies adopted were near enough nil – short of armed revolution. The more extreme socialists – such as the 'communist' group headed by Karl Marx and Friedrich Engels – recognized this and were frankly revolutionary. Marx always said that the socialist state wasn't going to be born because of a sudden upsurge of brotherly love but only after bitter warfare between the haves and have-nots. And by the have-nots Marx meant specifically the urban proletariat. While most historically minded intellectuals were looking at the way the middle classes were taking over from the upper classes, Marx looked beyond to the day when the industrial workers, the fastest-growing class in Europe, would take over from the middle class.

One of Marx's predictions was that the urban proletariat was going to get even poorer. This idea looked most convincing during down-turns in the business cycle such as the slump that began in 1846. As the factories closed, the number of people with literally nothing to lose climbed to levels that had everyone worried. In Paris, for example, 120,000 people, a third of the work force, were without jobs by the end of 1847.

1. Things were not so good in the other parts of the United Kingdom: the post-Reform Bill proportion in Scotland was one in eight, in Ireland one in twenty.

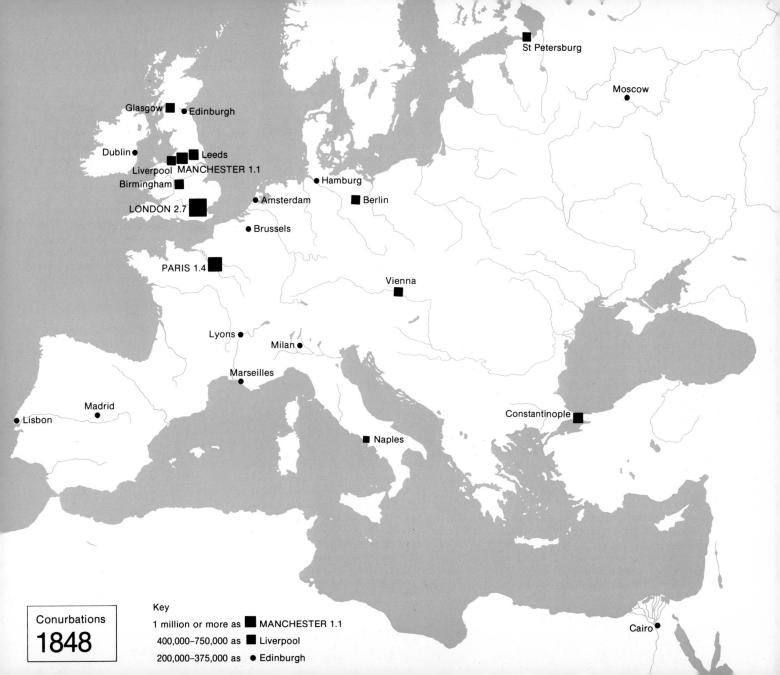

Glasgow
● Edinburgh

Dublin ●

Leeds

Liverpool   MANCHESTER 1.1

Birmingham

LONDON 2.7

● Amsterdam

● Brussels

St Petersburg

Moscow ●

Hamburg

Berlin

PARIS 1.4

Vienna

Lyons ●

Milan ●

Marseilles ●

Lisbon ●

Madrid ●

Naples

Constantinople

Cairo ●

Conurbations
1848

Key

1 million or more as ■ MANCHESTER 1.1

400,000–750,000 as ■ Liverpool

200,000–375,000 as ● Edinburgh

FROM THE START it was clear that 1848 was going to be a busy year. In January the Sicilians decided that they had had enough of being ruled from Naples and set up a provisional government of their own, while the death of the King of Denmark brought the Schleswig-Holstein problem a step nearer flash-point. In February there was more trouble, this time in France, and whereas neither Sicily nor Schleswig-Holstein was exactly at the centre of Europe's polity, France was its lynch-pin.

Despite his professed admiration for the British political system, Louis-Philippe had never really got the hang of being a constitutional monarch: behind the scenes he was always wheeling and dealing to keep his parliamentary protégés in power. This activity was quite unnecessary, for the mood of the country was deeply conservative, but he couldn't or wouldn't stop it and eventually he overdid it: his use of 'public order' as a pretext to ban the opposition party's entirely innocuous meetings became so manifestly unfair that it provoked serious riots in Paris. On the second day of the rioting (23 February) nervous troops let go with a volley, killing twenty. Activists paraded the dead round the city on an open cart and the next morning 100,000 angry citizens were on the streets. Barricades went up, the tricolour rose above them and a new generation of Frenchmen found themselves singing the Marseillaise. Louis-Philippe did the decent thing and gracefully lowered himself into the dustbin of history. As he left the Tuileries, a mixed bag of opposition deputies, left-wing journalists and socialist theoreticians appeared on the balcony of the Hôtel de Ville and proclaimed the Second Republic.

Paris cheered; Europe trembled. Was a new round of revolutionary wars about to begin? Better reform than revolution, said the wise, and kings and emperors suddenly found virtues in liberal politicians they had previously refused to talk to. In the single month of March, the Kings of Prussia, Holland and Piedmont-Sardinia, the Emperor of Austria and the Pope all agreed to grant liberal constitutions. Even more extraordinary, the German princes agreed to the calling of a national parliament, which actually came into existence at Frankfurt at the end of the month. From the Pyrenees to Poland – though not in Spain or Russia – liberalism was triumphant.

Nor was this all that happened in March. Italian patriotism scored its most spectacular successes yet with armed risings in Venice (17 March) and Milan (18–22 March); the Venetians then proclaimed a new Venetian Republic, while the Milanese called on King Charles Albert of Piedmont-Sardinia to take them under his protection. He accepted and declared war on Austria (24 March). On the same day the estates of Schleswig-Holstein formally renounced the Danish connection.

For the Austrian Empire the situation looked grim. The Hungarians were talking of seceding; the Czechs had called for a pan-Slav conference that could lead the same way; the rioters who had forced Metternich into exile were still on the streets in Vienna. Now the Italian states were in open revolt. In despair the Emperor Ferdinand II retired to Innsbruck, his only consolation the news that France, Austria's old enemy and a great one for meddling in Italian affairs, showed no sign of moving.

France was in truth in no condition to attack anyone. The revolutionary government, set up in February, had done two unprecedented things: given the vote to all nine million Frenchmen over twenty-one and begun welfare payments to the unemployed. In May the newly elected assembly met and took over power; to the surprise and anger of the left it proved to be a reactionary body, whose first act was to cut back on the welfare programme. On 23 June the Parisians rose again, this time against the republic. The rising was crushed in four days of fighting, which cost the lives of more Frenchmen than the February revolution. To add to the bitterness, several thousand captured rebels were shot in cold blood after organized resistance had ended.

Paris was not the only place where the revolutionary tide was ebbing. On 17 June the Austrian Army Commander in Bohemia, after a rather shaky start, managed to bring Prague under martial law: the threat of trouble from the Slavs immediately began to recede. In Italy, reinforcements got through to the Austrian Commander and he was able to go over to the offensive. On 27 July Charles Albert declared himself King of Upper Italy, a new entity uniting Piedmont-Sardinia, Parma, Modena and Milan. His announcement was less significant than the crushing defeat his army had sustained at Custozza two days before. The new kingdom was melting away even as it was proclaimed.

K. OF SWEDEN
AND NORWAY

UNITED
KINGDOM

K. OF
DENMARK

PROVISIONAL
GOVERNMENT OF
SCHLESWIG-HOLSTEIN

OF PRUSSIA

RUSSIAN EMPIRE

K. OF
HOLLAND

K. OF
BELGIUM

K.

MINOR
GERMAN
STATES

AUSTRIAN
EMPIRE

unsubdued
Circassians

FRENCH
REPUBLIC

SWISS

MOLDAVIA

K. OF
UPPER
ITALY

Custozza

VENETIAN
REPUBLIC

WALLACHIA

SERBIA

K. OF
PORTUGAL

TUSCANY

K. OF SPAIN

PAPAL
STATE

MONTENEGRO

OTTOMAN EMPIRE

K. OF NAPLES

Ionian
Islands
(BRITISH)

Gibraltar

BRITISH POSSESSIONS IN THE MEDITERRANEAN

K. OF GREECE

PROVISIONAL
GOVERNMENT
OF SICILY

K. OF MOROCCO

Algeria
(FRENCH)

BEYLIK OF
TUNIS

Malta

27 July
1848

VICEROYALTY OF
EGYPT

THE AUSTRIAN COMMANDER in Italy, Radetzky, followed up his victory over the Piedmontese with commendable vigour: by August 1848 he had bundled them back into their own territory and got their king's signature on a truce that restored the *status quo ante*. Not bad for an eighty year old, but then Radetzky had had a good teacher: he'd fought Napoleon over the same ground. News of his success put new heart into the government back in Vienna: the troops that had suppressed the dissidents in Prague were brought in to clear the streets of the capital, which they did so effectively that by the end of the year it seemed safe to send most of them off to fight the Hungarians. To make it clear that this fortunate turn of events marked the beginning of a new era, a Habsburg family conclave forced the inadequate Emperor Ferdinand II off the throne and put his nephew, young Franz Joseph, in his place.

But Austria's troubles weren't over yet. The invasion of Hungary ended in humiliating failure and by early 1849 the whole country, bar a few fortresses, was under the control of the patriot leader Kossuth. In Italy, the Venetian Republic proved impossible to reduce and when Rome and Tuscany also declared themselves republics, which they did in early March, King Charles Albert of Piedmont-Sardinia was encouraged to try his luck again. It hadn't improved: at Novara, on the Piedmontese side of the frontier, Radetzky caught him wrong-footed and he was beaten as badly as he had been at Custozza. Still, despite this victory, Austria's overall position was barely holding steady. Franz Joseph had to ignore the Pope's appeals for help against the Roman Republic and make his own appeal to the Tsar. This was successful: Russian contingents soon arrived to join the Austrian forces on the borders of Hungary.

Help for the Pope came from an unlikely source, the French. In December 1848 the French Republic had held its first presidential election, the candidates being Louis Napoleon (a son of Napoleon's brother Louis) and Marshal Cavaignac (the soldier responsible for suppressing the socialist revolt in Paris in June); to no one's surprise Louis Napoleon proved an easy winner. His name was his greatest asset, of course, but he was also a clever politician in his own right: since his first aim was to win the support of the Royalist-Catholic bloc, he authorized the dispatch of an army corps to Rome. This sailed for Italy in April and was at the gates of Rome by the end of the month. There, to the astonishment of all concerned, the advance guard suffered a sharp defeat. Garibaldi and his Italian Legion were out to prove that the French Commander's comment – 'Italians don't fight' – didn't apply to them.

Garibaldi held Rome for a month. He couldn't win and, in truth, he didn't even direct the battle very well – he was always better at a war of movement than a formal siege – but he did get Italians to die for Italy. When the end came, he and his legion still refused to surrender. On the eve of capitulation he led his men out of the city, the idea being to make a fighting retreat across the Apennines to Venice. It proved impossibly far. Most of the legionaries gave up at San Marino, the hill-top republic whose neutrality the Austrians had to respect; most of the rest died when the Austrians intercepted their squadron of commandeered fishing boats off the Adriatic coast. Garibaldi was rescued by the local peasantry and smuggled away, eventually to America.

For the moment it was all over. The Tuscan republic had collapsed in April, Sicily had been reconquered by the Neapolitans in May, Hungary was recovered for the Habsburg Empire by the combined forces of Austria and Russia in August, and at the end of that month the Venetian Republic, which had successfully withstood Radetzky's bombardment, finally succumbed to famine.

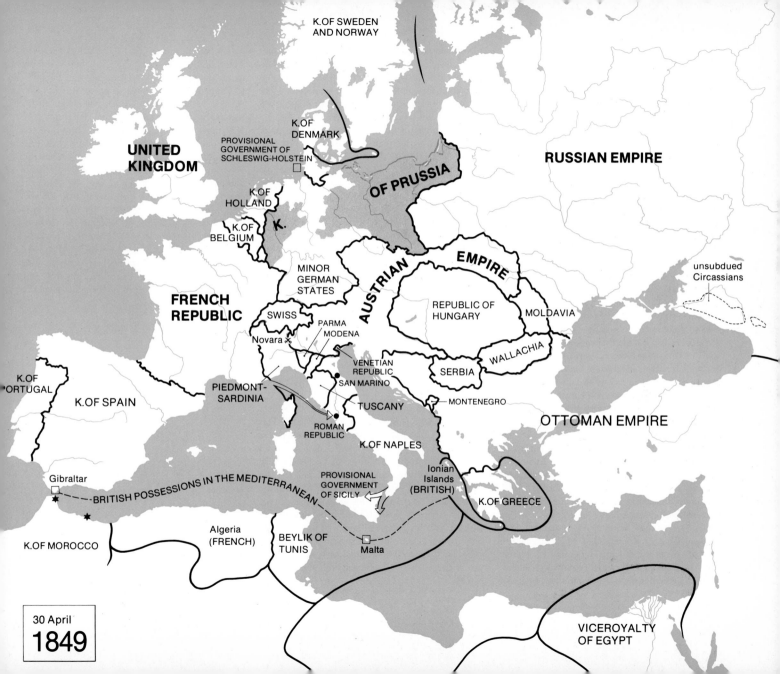

K.OF SWEDEN
AND NORWAY

K.OF
DENMARK

UNITED
KINGDOM

PROVISIONAL
GOVERNMENT OF
SCHLESWIG-HOLSTEIN

RUSSIAN EMPIRE

OF PRUSSIA

K.OF
HOLLAND

K.
K.OF
BELGIUM

MINOR
GERMAN
STATES

AUSTRIAN   EMPIRE

unsubdued
Circassians

FRENCH
REPUBLIC

SWISS

PARMA
MODENA

Novara ✕

REPUBLIC OF
HUNGARY

MOLDAVIA

VENETIAN
REPUBLIC

SAN MARINO

WALLACHIA

K.OF
PORTUGAL

K.OF SPAIN

PIEDMONT-
SARDINIA

TUSCANY

SERBIA

MONTENEGRO

OTTOMAN EMPIRE

ROMAN
REPUBLIC

K.OF NAPLES

Gibraltar

★

★

BRITISH POSSESSIONS IN THE MEDITERRANEAN

PROVISIONAL
GOVERNMENT
OF SICILY

Ionian
Islands
(BRITISH)

K.OF GREECE

K.OF MOROCCO

Algeria
(FRENCH)

BEYLIK OF
TUNIS

Malta

VICEROYALTY
OF EGYPT

30 April
1849

AT THE PEAK of the 1848–9 wave of pan-German patriotism the Frankfurt parliament had offered King Frederick William IV of Prussia the chance of becoming Emperor of Germany. Frederick the Great would have leapt at it; Frederick William backed away. Obsessed with the idea of legitimacy, he only wanted the imperial crown if it was offered by the princes, not the people (and the princes had more sense); in the same way, convinced of the soundness of the Danish king's claim to Schleswig-Holstein, he stood aside and let the Danes reconquer the Duchies (1850–52). Most extraordinary of all, he allowed the Austrians to extort from him a promise not to set up anything like the *Zollverein* in the political sphere but to recognize the do-nothing confederation as the sole pan-German organization. No wonder most Prussians referred to this convention, signed at Olmutz at the end of 1850, as 'the capitulation of Olmutz'.

Louis Napoleon, unlike Frederick William, knew how to make use of his opportunities. His four-year term as President of the French Republic was due to end in 1852 and a second term was specifically forbidden by the constitution; he sensed, however, that the country wouldn't protest if he seized power, as he did in a bloodless administrative coup at the end of 1851. The next year he proclaimed himself Emperor under the title of Napoleon III; the French people, as he had guessed, endorsed both actions.

At first the new Emperor was cold-shouldered by the royal families of Europe who didn't see much to choose between Bonapartism and Republicanism. The news of his coup went down particularly badly in London: Queen Victoria made no secret of the fact that she looked on Louis Napoleon as a usurper and an opportunist; her ministers feared that under his leadership France would start a new round of military adventuring. Karl Marx, also a Londoner now (after 1848 no continental country would have him), was equally opposed: he lampooned Louis as a

pantomime king making a trivial attempt to turn back the clock of history. But although Marx forecast a short reign, events elsewhere gave Louis Napoleon the chance to become respectable. The Russians were moving in on Constantinople and it was going to take all Europe to stop them.

The harmony of Europe depended on the major powers resisting temptation. Prussia had just set a splendid example of the sort of self-control – or pusillanimity – required by resisting the temptation to lead the German people into one Reich. Russia's temptation was Constantinople and, as every year Turkey got weaker, so every year the temptation got stronger. In 1853 Tsar Nicholas I succumbed. An ultimatum delivered in April demanded that the Sultan recognize the right of Russia to represent and protect his Christian subjects. This was, in effect, demanding a protectorate over Turkey itself and, after consulting with the British and French ambassadors, the Sultan returned a firm No. The British and French Mediterranean fleets assembled in the Dardanelles, the Russians occupied Moldavia and Wallachia, Turkey declared war on Russia and conflict between the major powers became inevitable when the Russian Black Sea Squadron moved out and destroyed the Turkish fleet (in November, off Sinope).

The first job of the British and French was to bolster up the Turkish position in the Balkans. This they did by intimidating the Greeks (who were thinking of joining in on the Russian side) and landing an expeditionary force at Gallipoli (April 1854). Russia's discomfiture was then completed by Franz Joseph of Austria, who told Nicholas he would join the Anglo-French coalition if the Russian troops in Wallachia and Moldavia weren't withdrawn immediately. Fuming – it was, after all, only five years since he had saved Franz Joseph's bacon in Hungary – Nicholas agreed to pull his army out. In every sense, he was now back where he had started.

Not that this meant that the war was over. The Allies felt they could hardly go home without fighting a battle and if the Russians wouldn't come to them they would have to go to Russia. They decided to land in the Crimea and blow up the Russian navy's installations at Sebastopol. In September they put ashore and marched on Sebastopol; a Russian force that tried to block their way was pushed aside (at the Battle of the Alma) and Sebastopol duly invested. Unfortunately, the Allies didn't have enough troops to seal off Sebastopol completely and, though they defeated the Russian field army's attacks on them (at Balaclava in October and at Inkerman in November), they made no progress with the siege. Nor had they made any provision against the Russian winter. The Tsar, who had said all along that his best generals were Generals January and February, watched with satisfaction as the strength of the Allies began to ebb.

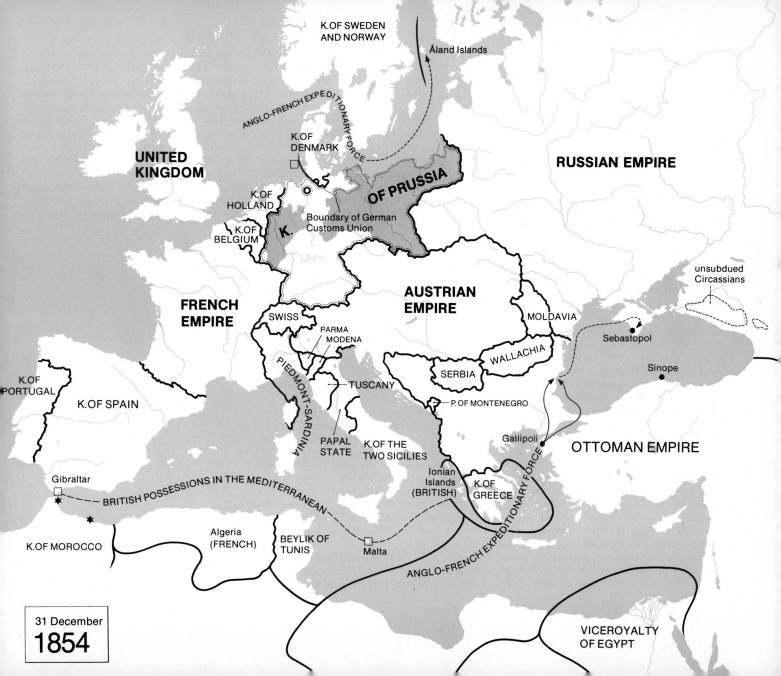

K. OF SWEDEN
AND NORWAY

Åland Islands

RUSSIAN EMPIRE

UNITED
KINGDOM

ANGLO-FRENCH EXPEDITIONARY FORCE

K. OF
DENMARK

K. OF
HOLLAND

K.

OF PRUSSIA

Boundary of German
Customs Union

K. OF
BELGIUM

FRENCH
EMPIRE

AUSTRIAN
EMPIRE

SWISS

MOLDAVIA

PARMA
MODENA

unsubdued
Circassians

Sebastopol

WALLACHIA

TUSCANY

Sinope

PIEDMONT-SARDINIA

SERBIA

K. OF
PORTUGAL

K. OF SPAIN

PAPAL
STATE

K. OF THE
TWO SICILIES

P. OF MONTENEGRO

Gallipoli

OTTOMAN EMPIRE

ANGLO-FRENCH EXPEDITIONARY FORCE

Gibraltar

BRITISH POSSESSIONS IN THE MEDITERRANEAN

Ionian
Islands
(BRITISH)

K. OF
GREECE

K. OF MOROCCO

Algeria
(FRENCH)

BEYLIK OF
TUNIS

Malta

31 December
1854

VICEROYALTY
OF EGYPT

THE WINTER OF 1854–5 reduced the Allied army in the Crimea to a state where it could do little more than defend itself; despite all the efforts made to improve its support services, rebuilding it took most of the next campaigning season. The French made a better job of this than the British, as was evident when the Allied offensive was resumed: it was a French assault that carried the redoubt on which the defence of Sebastopol hinged and forced the Russians to evacuate the city (September 1855). The Tsar's army was the one with the supply problem now – Russia was still almost without railways – and this, combined with more threats from ungrateful Austria, persuaded him to agree to peace negotiations. These took a long time (from December 1855 to March 1856) and the most important consequence of them, the union of Moldavia and Wallachia to form the state of Romania, wasn't actually consummated until 1858, but the fact that Russia was prepared to abandon her Balkan ambitions was clear from the start. The Tsar agreed to pull back from the lower Danube, yielding the delta to the Turks and a slice of Bessarabia to Moldavia: more important, he also renounced the right to enter Romania at will.[1]

Among the signatories of the treaty that confirmed all these arrangements was Cavour, Prime Minister of Piedmont. He had joined the Allies in the hope that they would make some gesture in favour of Italian unity. Gestures were all he got, which sharpened his thinking remarkably: he saw that he had to be more specific about what he wanted and what he was prepared to give. The nub of the problem was that the Italians weren't able to get the Austrians out of Italy by their own efforts, so someone else would have to do it for them. That someone could only be Napoleon III. In 1858 Cavour and Napoleon met in secret and the two of them hammered out a programme: Cavour would provoke an Austrian invasion in early 1859,

Napoleon would hurry to the rescue and the French army would then conquer Lombardy and Venetia. In return for these provinces – and the opportunity to 'liberate' Parma, Modena and the Romagna (the northernmost province of the Papal State) – Cavour would give Napoleon Savoy and Nice (the parts of Piedmont on the French side of the Alps).

Cavour engineered the outbreak of war the next year exactly on schedule and Napoleon duly arrived in Italy to assume the most demanding of all the roles thrust on him by the Napoleonic legend, that of old Mars himself. He made a reasonable start. The French army was concentrated on the Austrians' left (because most of it had landed at Genoa); Napoleon moved it north, across the Austrian front, and drove the Austrian army out of its position by outflanking its right. The battle of Magenta wasn't a very sanguinary affair, but it did force the Austrians out of Lombardy and allow Napoleon to make a triumphal entry into Milan. He was the hero of the hour.

Cavour was also happy. After Magenta, local patriots stimulated the inhabitants of Parma, Modena and the Romagna into asking for annexation to Piedmont. A similar request from the Tuscans, who had expelled their Duke and voted for a provisional union with Piedmont on the eve of the war, could not be accepted, because Tuscany hadn't formed part of the agreement with Napoleon; but if the French Emperor could finish off the campaign as well as he had started it, the failures of 1848–9 would be redeemed and the Kingdom of Upper Italy established on a sure foundation.

The end of the campaign was closer than Cavour thought. The Austrians had received reinforcements and recovered confidence. Franz Joseph arrived on the scene, took personal command of operations and ordered an immediate counter-offensive. The result was that the French and Austrian armies blundered into each other at Solferino, just south of Lake Garda. At the end of a long and bloody day the

French had possession of the battlefield but were almost as completely fought out as the Austrians. Their supply situation was even worse. Napoleon, who had already been having second thoughts about his commitment to liberate Venetia, decided to call a halt. He was genuinely horrified by the slaughter, news was coming in of Prussia mobilizing in support of Austria, and all his political instincts told him not to get involved in a long war. Let Piedmont keep Nice and Savoy, he was going home. Two weeks after Solferino Napoleon and Franz Joseph signed an armistice which gave Lombardy to Piedmont but otherwise left things as they had been before the war.

1. The Russians also agreed to return Kars in Trans-Caucasia to the Turks (they had captured it the year before) and to the neutralization of the Aland Islands in the Baltic (which the British had taken in 1854).

CAVOUR RESIGNED in fury when he heard that Napoleon and Franz Joseph had agreed to a truce, but there was no real need for him to be so upset: the Austrian hegemony over the peninsula had gone forever and, whatever might be said about legal rights, no one was going to put the Dukes of Parma, Modena and Tuscany back on their thrones or restore the authority of the Pope in the Romagna. By the beginning of 1860 Cavour had seen this and was back at work arranging for plebiscites to be held in these provinces. Napoleon, a great believer in plebiscites, was forced to accept the results, which were 95 per cent or more in favour of union with Piedmont. His agreement, though, cost Cavour the price originally agreed for Venetia, i.e. Nice and Savoy.

All these arrangements took until May to complete; while they were in progress, Cavour was on tenterhooks lest the Powers intervene and put a stop to them. What he needed was a calm and orderly transfer of power in the northern provinces and a period of total tranquillity elsewhere in the peninsula. What he got was Garibaldi landing in Sicily proclaiming that he and his legion were going to bring all Italy under Piedmontese rule.

Garibaldi, still the only Italian soldier to have acquired any distinction to date, had been behaving increasingly erratically since the end of the Solferino campaign. The cession of Nice, his home town, had understandably enraged him and he felt entirely out of sympathy with Cavour's salami-slicing approach to Italian unity. But his attempts to found a political party of his own only made him look foolish and a brief marriage to a seventeen-year-old girl (he was fifty-two at the time) didn't help either. When he heard that the Sicilians had risen in revolt he decided to commit his volunteer force to their cause.

There wasn't a word of truth in the reports. Garibaldi and his thousand legionaries landed at the western end of the island – after successfully eluding the Piedmontese and Sicilian squadrons trying to intercept them – to find that they were entirely on their own. Undeterred, they set out for the capital, Palermo. Half-way there they came up against a force of 3,000 regulars equipped with rifles (Garibaldi's men had only muskets), holding a hill that commanded the road. Garibaldi knew this was a battle that he had to win head on. He and his men fought their way up the hill terrace by terrace until they were in a position to carry it with one last rush; though they had no more ammunition – nor, for that matter, any food or water – they did it, and the victory was plain to see. Cheering Sicilians fell in behind Garibaldi's column as it resumed the march on Palermo.

Palermo had a garrison of 24,000. Garibaldi drew off a few thousand by a feint from the south followed by what was apparently a retreat, then he slipped into the city by night from the east. His weakness – he still had less than 4,000 men – was concealed by the governor's decision to bombard the city before counter-attacking; in the resulting confusion Garibaldi was able to rouse the citizenry and build the barricades he needed for a successful defence. Three days later the governor asked for a truce; a week after that he agreed to evacuate the city and ship his men back to Naples.

The rest of Sicily fell to Garibaldi without much fighting and by early August his army, now 12,000 strong, was ready to tackle the mainland. His proclamations still declared his intention of uniting Italy under the crown of Piedmont, but his personal sentiments and those of most of his followers were known to be republican: Cavour felt it would be highly dangerous to let him rule the south for a moment longer than was necessary. The time had come for the Piedmontese army to march on Naples. The trouble was that the only way it could reach Naples was through the Papal State and this would precipitate lip-pursing diplomatic problems. Napoleon wouldn't let the Piedmontese march through Rome, but would he allow them to take the Adriatic route? Napoleon's reply filtered back as an ambassador's whisper, 'Do it, but do it quickly.'

Piedmontese armies never moved very fast and this one was still getting itself organized when Garibaldi slipped across the straits of Messina, took Reggio and moved on Naples. The closer he got to the city, the faster resistance crumbled: the last King of the Two Sicilies left his capital without making any attempt to fight for it. Garibaldi arrived the next day, by train. A hundred miles to the north the Pope was reading an ultimatum from Cavour. When he rejected it, the Piedmontese immediately invaded his Adriatic provinces. At the battle of Castelfidardo the papal forces were overwhelmed – after many years as a poetic aspiration Italian unity had suddenly become a reality.

K. OF SWEDEN
AND NORWAY

UNITED
KINGDOM

K. OF DENMARK

RUSSIAN EMPIRE

OF PRUSSIA

K. OF
HOLLAND

K. OF
BELGIUM

K.

MINOR
GERMAN
STATES

FRENCH
EMPIRE

SWISS

AUSTRIAN
EMPIRE

Savoy

unsubdued
Circassians

ROMANIA

SERBIA

Nice

K. OF
PORTUGAL

K. OF SPAIN

✕ Castelfidardo

P. OF MONTENEGRO

OTTOMAN EMPIRE

K. OF PIEDMONT-SARDINIA

PAPAL
STATE

K. OF THE
TWO SICILIES

Gibraltar

Gaeta
Naples

Ionian
Islands
(BRITISH)

Garibaldi

BRITISH POSSESSIONS

Palermo

K. OF GREECE

K. OF MOROCCO

Algeria
(FRENCH)

BEYLIK OF
TUNIS

Malta

VICEROYALTY
OF EGYPT

18 September
1860

At THE END OF 1863 Frederick VII of Denmark died and the question of Schleswig-Holstein came up again. This time there was no fudging the issue: the people of the Duchies wanted to be free and they had every right to be; the legal heir to the Duchies was the Duke of Augustenborg, not the new King of Denmark. When the Danes made it clear that, be this as it may, they wouldn't give up without a fight, the German Confederation was momentarily nonplussed: it had a war on its hands but no army with which to fight it. All it could do was ask its two senior members, Franz Joseph of Austria and William I, the new King of Prussia, to invade the Duchies on the Confederation's behalf, trusting that when they had conquered them they would turn them over to Augustenborg.

Franz Joseph of Austria and William of Prussia were trustworthy, but King William's Prime Minister, Bismarck, was not. He was scheming to get the Duchies for Prussia. He couldn't annex them by unilateral military action, of course, as the Prussian army could only move in the name of Germany. Yet acting as an agent of the Confederation would mean losing political control of the operation. Bismarck's solution to this dilemma was to engineer a quarrel between the Confederation on the one hand and Austria and Prussia, who were providing the invading army, on the other. Consequently, in the brief German-Danish War of 1864, Austria and Prussia fought without commitments except to each other and it was to the two of them 'jointly' that the Danes finally ceded the Duchies. At this stage everyone, including Franz Joseph and William I, still thought the Duchies ought to go to Augustenborg, but Bismarck managed to keep the talks about this going on long enough for everyone to get used to other ideas – partition between Austria and Prussia, for example. In 1865 it turned out that joint administration of Schleswig-Holstein was causing so many problems that a division along

these lines was actually put into effect – purely as an interim measure, of course. Prussia got Schleswig, Austria Holstein. It didn't take the Austrians long to wake up to the fact that Holstein was no use to them at all and in 1866 they threw the whole question back to the Confederation. In doing so they breached the 1864 agreement with Prussia, and Bismarck was able to present himself as the injured party when he declared war. He offset the fact that a majority of the Confederation was on Austria's side by encouraging the Italians to attack Austria's southern frontier.[1]

Considering that the Austro-Prussian War involved two major powers and several minor ones, it was surprisingly short, sharp and decisive: it lasted only seven weeks altogether. Credit for this is traditionally and quite correctly given to the Chief of the Prussian General Staff, General Moltke, whose plan for a converging attack on Bohemia by three armies couldn't have gone better. The Austrians completely missed their chance of taking on the Prussian armies one at a time; when they did decide to stand their ground – at Sadowa, three weeks after the outbreak of hostilities – Moltke had his three armies close enough together to fight in the same battle. The Army of the Elbe (E) and I Army attacked the Austrians head on, then II Army rolled up their right flank. It was the decisive victory Moltke had planned for – and he followed it up perfectly too. Within three weeks the Prussians were at the gates of Vienna; a week after that they had Franz Joseph agreeing to peace.

The other campaigns of the Seven Weeks War had no effect on its course or on the peace that concluded it. The scratch Prussian corps sent against the hostile members of the German Confederation proved adequate for its tasks – the occupation of Hanover and the defeat of Baden, Württemberg and Bavaria. The Austrians trounced the Italians by land (at Custozza again) and sea (off Lissa), but they still had to cede Venetia to them.

A final point to be noted on this map is Greece's acquisition of the Ionian Islands. The British had decided that the naval base on Malta was sufficient for their needs in this area and they turned the Islands over to the Greek authorities in 1864.

1. The Kingdom of Italy had been formally constituted in 1861 after plebiscites in the Kingdom of the Two Sicilies and the Papal States (bar the Patrimonium, still held for the Pope by two French regiments). The Italians were now after Venetia; though Napoleon III had told them that, in the present emergency, he could get it for them for nothing, they insisted on going about it the hard way.

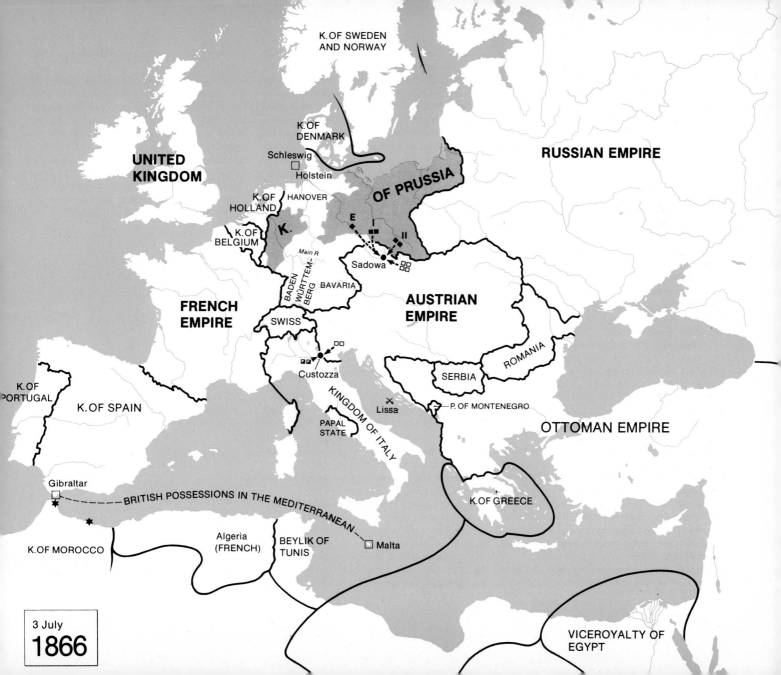

K. OF SWEDEN
AND NORWAY

RUSSIAN EMPIRE

UNITED
KINGDOM

K. OF
DENMARK

Schleswig

Holstein

K. OF
HOLLAND

HANOVER

OF PRUSSIA

K. OF
BELGIUM

K.

E

II

Main R.

Sadowa

BADEN
WÜRTTEM-
BERG

BAVARIA

FRENCH
EMPIRE

AUSTRIAN
EMPIRE

SWISS

ROMANIA

Custozza

SERBIA

K. OF
PORTUGAL

K. OF SPAIN

Lissa

P. OF MONTENEGRO

OTTOMAN EMPIRE

PAPAL
STATE

KINGDOM OF ITALY

Gibraltar

BRITISH POSSESSIONS IN THE MEDITERRANEAN

K. OF GREECE

Malta

K. OF MOROCCO

Algeria
(FRENCH)

BEYLIK OF
TUNIS

VICEROYALTY OF
EGYPT

3 July
1866

AFTER THE SEVEN WEEKS WAR there could be no doubt as to who was master in Germany. Prussia got not only the Duchies that had been the official cause of the dispute, Schleswig and Holstein, but also the territories of five of her opponents: Hanover, Nassau, Hesse-Cassel, Hesse-Homburg and Frankfurt. Moreover, all the remaining states north of the Main were forced to join a North German Confederation, which gave Prussia effective control of their affairs. Of the thirty-five small to medium-sized states in the old confederation (now dissolved), only Bavaria, Württemberg, Baden, Luxembourg and Hesse-Darmstadt (*HD* on the map) retained full sovereignty. Bismarck and Moltke between them had obtained for King William five million new subjects, the allegiance of another five millions and the equivalent of three extra army corps.[1]

Bismarck's next trick was exceptionally neat. The King of Holland wanted to sell Luxembourg, Napoleon wanted to buy it and Bismarck had promised not to oppose the deal if France kept out of the Seven Weeks War. But when news of the proposed purchase leaked out, there was an immediate outcry in Germany. Luxembourg had been a member of the old confederation and, whether or not it was included in Bismarck's new one, it was intolerable to pan-German sentiment that it should pass under French rule. Bismarck had to tell Napoleon that he couldn't, after all, agree to the transaction; all he could do was allow Luxembourg to be neutralized, like Belgium. The real bonus for Bismarck – who had, of course, done nothing to discourage the pan-German trumpetings that characterized the affair – was that the south German states had agreed to put their armies at Prussia's disposal in the event of war with France. This gave Moltke the equivalent of three more corps.

Prussia could now field an army twice the size of France's, a fact which did not escape Napoleon's attention: he can hardly have forgotten the old French saying about God being on the side of the big battalions. But when he tried to persuade his generals to change to the Prussian system of universal military service he met with a point blank refusal: if there was money available, they said, it ought to be spent buying breech-loading rifles for the regular forces. When the armies of Europe had switched over from the musket to the rifle in the 1840s and 50s, the French, like nearly everyone else, had opted for a muzzle-loading weapon: the Prussians' choice of a breech-loader was considered highly eccentric. The Seven Weeks War had demonstrated beyond doubt that the Prussians had been right: for every shot the Austrian rifleman had fired from his muzzle-loader, the Prussian with his breech-loader had fired six. It was to this crushing tactical advantage (not Moltke's strategy) that the French ascribed Prussia's success and breech-loaders were what they wanted before anything else.

The French certainly acted on this assessment: between 1866 and 1870, they produced a million breech-loaders of a better design than the Prussian one. If the speed was remarkable, the need for it was obvious: the two countries were clearly moving towards war.

It was France that forced the issue. In 1870 the Spanish throne, vacant since a liberal revolution in 1868, was offered to a Prussian prince. The French refused to accept the Prussian king's word that the offer had been turned down as a sufficient reassurance; they demanded that the king declare that the candidature would never be resumed. When this demand was ignored, they declared war.

Bismarck did what he could to help this exchange along: war with France was clearly the quickest way to bring the rest of Germany into the Prussian camp. As to the military outcome, he never seems to have had any doubt at all. In this, of course, he was only taking the same view as most Germans, but opinion outside Germany favoured the French. Not only

was the French army entirely professional; it had a Napoleon to lead it.

This was perhaps not quite the advantage it had been. As many ladies of the court could testify, Louis Napoleon had thoroughly enjoyed his eighteen years as Emperor. Unfortunately, his campaigns in the boudoir had left his genito-urinary system so ravaged that he was no longer really fit for campaigns in the country. The army was looking for the son of Austerlitz, or at least for the man of Magenta. What it got was a semi-invalid who found it agonizing to sit astride a horse and quite impossible to make any sort of decision.

1. Counting Prussia, the North German Confederation had twenty members; the kingdoms of Prussia and Saxony, the four Saxon duchies (*SD* on the map), the two Mecklenburg duchies (*ME*), the Duchies of Brunswick (*DB*) and Oldenburg (*OL*), the three free cities of Lübeck (*Lüb*), Hamburg (*Ham*) and Bremen (*Brem*) and seven other mini states (not shown). All these states were in the Customs Union bar Bremen and Hamburg which didn't join until the 1880s.

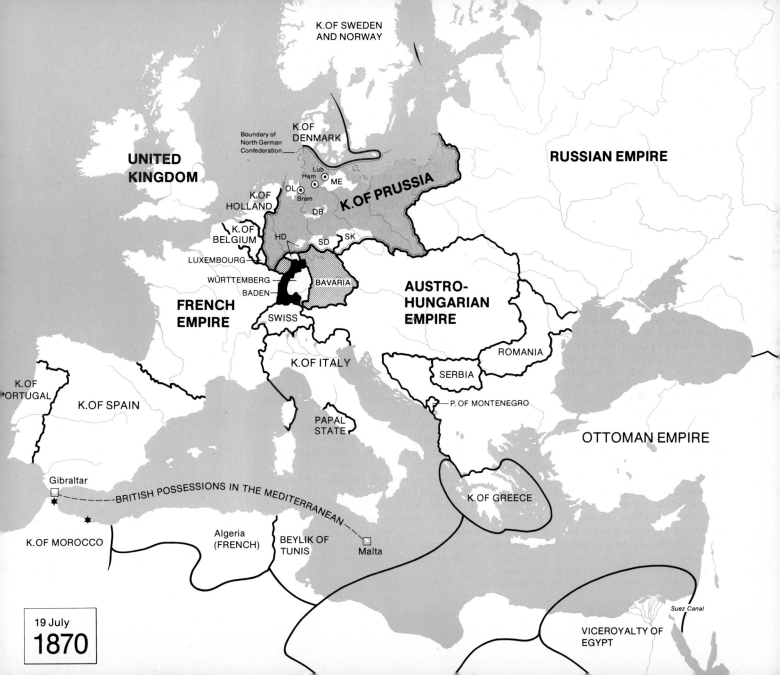

UNITED
KINGDOM

K.OF SWEDEN
AND NORWAY

RUSSIAN EMPIRE

Boundary of
North German
Confederation

K.OF
DENMARK

Lub
Ham
ME
OL
Brem
K.OF
HOLLAND
DB
K.OF
BELGIUM
HD
SD
SK
Luxembourg
WÜRTTEMBERG
BADEN
BAVARIA
FRENCH
EMPIRE
SWISS

K.OF PRUSSIA

AUSTRO-
HUNGARIAN
EMPIRE

ROMANIA

SERBIA

K.OF ITALY

P. OF MONTENEGRO

K.OF
PORTUGAL
K.OF SPAIN

PAPAL
STATE

OTTOMAN EMPIRE

Gibraltar
BRITISH POSSESSIONS IN THE MEDITERRANEAN

K.OF GREECE

K.OF MOROCCO
Algeria
(FRENCH)
BEYLIK OF
TUNIS
Malta

Suez Canal

VICEROYALTY OF
EGYPT

19 July
1870

WITHIN THREE WEEKS of receiving the French declaration of war Moltke had fourteen of his fifteen corps on the stretch of the Franco-German frontier between the Moselle and the Rhine. The French army, which consisted of eight corps, had six forward. Each side deployed its main strength to the left, so the German superiority – overall two to one – became four to one at the right end of the French line. These were decisive odds: the French corps here was forced back as soon as the fighting began and indeed was so badly mauled in the opening battle (at Worth on 6 August) that it had to be withdrawn altogether. The other right-wing corps soon shared its fate, leaving the road to central France wide open.

As the Germans moved forward, the French left had to retreat too, but it did so in good order, reaching its main base, the fortress of Metz, without significant loss. However, its five corps couldn't be expected to halt the German advance by themselves; a minimum of eight or nine corps would be needed to do that. Napoleon handed over command to Marshal Bazaine and hurried back to Chalons, where the right wing was being reconstituted. A newly raised corps brought the strength of this 'Army of Chalons' to four corps; Napoleon, who had given up the pretence of directing operations himself, entrusted it to Marshal MacMahon. The idea was for Bazaine to fall back on Chalons and for the two Marshals to use their combined nine corps for some masterly, though as yet unformulated, counterstroke.

Unfortunately Bazaine stayed in Metz too long. By the time he started to pull out on 14 August, German columns were already moving parallel to his, the nearest of them only a dozen miles to the south. On the 16th, at Rezonville, there was an accidental battle which made the situation clear to everyone; by the 18th Moltke had eight corps across the French line of retreat. On that day the bloody Battle of Gravelotte showed Bazaine that he wasn't going to be able to fight his way back to Chalons: if the French armies were to be united, MacMahon would have to come to him.

MacMahon, accompanied by a grey-faced Napoleon, duly set out from Chalons on the 21st. By the 25th Moltke had a shrewd idea where this French force was, and the German armies not involved in shepherding Bazaine back to Metz began to wheel north to head it off. On the 29th they found MacMahon's right flank and on the 30th forced him off his line of march. He halted at the town of Sedan, intending to rest up and then try again, but while he was preparing his general order for the next day ('Repos aujourd'hui pour toute l'armée'), his corps commanders were marking up the Prussian campfires on their maps. They made a complete circle round the town.

Early the next morning Moltke established his headquarters on a hillside with a good view of Sedan and he, King William and Bismarck settled down to watch. It didn't take long. By the evening the fighting had ended and negotiations were in progress for the formal surrender of the entire French force. A hundred thousand Frenchmen were to become prisoners of war, among them Louis Napoleon. The pantomime of the Second Empire was over.

The Second Empire was replaced by the Third Republic, proclaimed by the people of Paris as soon as they heard the news of Sedan. In the accompanying euphoria the idea somehow got around that the Prussians would now go home and leave the French to work out their new destiny. The truth was far different. Bismarck didn't care whether the French were ruled by an emperor, a king or a cabinet, peace was going to cost them dear. By the time the Parisians had accepted this ugly fact, the Prussian armies were at the gates of the city. Indeed,

(continued overleaf)

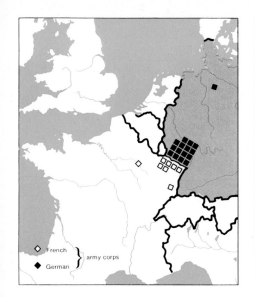

MacMahon at
Chalons

Bazaine at Metz

I II
III

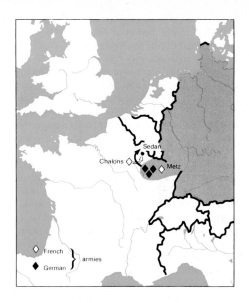

Sedan
Chalons   Metz

1 August 1870
THE INITIAL DEPLOYMENT

20 August 1870
THE GERMAN INVASION

2 September 1870
SEDAN

THE FRANCO-PRUSSIAN WAR: OPENING PHASE

they had drawn their siege lines; Gambetta, the leading spirit of the new republic, had to leave the capital by balloon.

Gambetta's plan was to raise enormous conscript armies in the provinces and simply sweep the Germans out of the country. It was true that Moltke, with half his forces committed to the siege of Paris and most of the rest watching Bazaine in Metz, had little with which to meet a counter-offensive, let alone a massive one. On the other hand Gambetta needed time to turn his conscripts into soldiers. Miracles of improvisation produced an 'Army of the Loire' of four corps by the beginning of November and a preliminary demonstration by this force persuaded the Germans to pull back from Orleans. But when it came to real battles there was a world of difference between the raw French levies and the battle-hardened German troops. The Army of the Loire's attempt to drive north and relieve Paris was easily held, as was the Paris garrison's attempt to break out to meet the relieving force (at the end of November): neither caused Moltke to lose a moment's sleep. He didn't even have to use the forces set free by the capitulation of Metz the month before.

Moltke's plan for Paris was simply to starve it out. This would obviously take time and Bismarck, worried by the fact that opinion in Europe was now moving in France's favour, pressed for a bombardment. He got his way and the guns duly opened up on 5 January 1871. But they did so to very little effect and Paris surrendered on 28 January simply because it had only ten days' food left. The armistice was extended to the rest of France three days later.

Temporarily excluded from this armistice were the departments near the Swiss frontier. The French government had reports that an attempt to relieve Belfort by their 'Army of the East' was going well and, desperately needing a success, they demanded that this battle be fought to its conclusion. It proved to be a fiasco, with most of the 150,000 Frenchmen involved getting pushed into Switzerland and interned.

So Bismarck had no difficulty imposing the peace terms he had always intended: the cession of Alsace and Lorraine and an indemnity of five billion francs. But the real prize was already his. Ten days before the surrender of Paris, in a carefully orchestrated ceremony at the Palace of Versailles, the German princes had hailed the King of Prussia as their overlord. As the French Empire passed into history, modern Germany entered its imperial epoch: before a beaming Bismarck, King William of Prussia was reborn as the first Kaiser of the Second Reich.[1]

1. The First Reich was what we term the Holy Roman Empire.

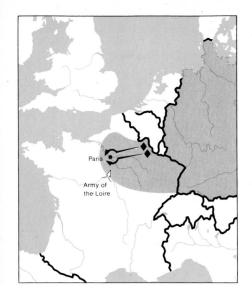 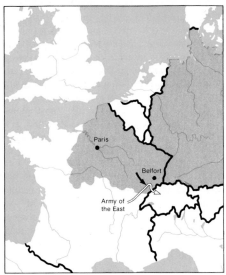 

1 December 1870
PARIS BESIEGED

31 January 1871
THE ARMISTICE

(apart from the French army attempting the relief of Belfort)

1 March 1871
THE PEACE

THE FRANCO-PRUSSIAN WAR: CONCLUDING PHASE

WHEN IT WAS CLEAR that Paris was going to be besieged, the city authorities, acting in the best revolutionary tradition, issued arms to the people. This didn't make any difference to the military situation, but it made everyone feel better – everyone, that is, except the Parisian bourgeoisie who were more frightened of the working class than they were of the Germans. And indeed the justification for the National Guard was entirely social: its exercises occupied the indigent, its rations sustained them and its meagre pay gave them a glimpse of security. The trouble came with the peace, the subsequent political reaction and the first moves towards demobilization – specifically with the new government's blundering attempt to deprive the Guard of its artillery. The officers sent to get the guns were lynched by an angry mob, which then swept down on the Hôtel de Ville. Surprisingly, it met no opposition. The ministers of the Third Republic had decided to abandon their unruly capital and leave the Commune of Paris, for the moment at least, to the rebels and their devices. These added up to a reasonably coherent socialist programme, the first ever enacted in Europe (March 1871).

The government's retreat was more sensible than it seemed. It had the overwhelming support of the country (it had only been elected the month before, so there is no doubt about this) and, once re-established at Versailles, the regular army rallied to it. While the Commune published its manifestos, the Republic gathered its forces; by April Paris was under siege again and by mid-May it was under assault. It took barely a week for the government's soldiers to pen the rebels up in the north-east corner of the city; the final battle there was a one-sided affair in which the Communards were massacred whether they surrendered or not.

The Commune's disastrous end confirmed Karl Marx in his low opinion of socialists: they simply weren't hard-headed enough to run a successful revolution. On the other hand, it turned many socialists away from violence and towards the ballot box. There was some evidence that this was indeed the path of the future. The franchise had been widened in Britain in 1867, where one in three adult males now had the vote. In Piedmont, the Netherlands, Denmark and Prussia, the constitutions granted in 1848 had survived the reaction and, as a result, a proportion of the adult male population that varied from under 10 per cent (Piedmont) to near enough 100 per cent (Prussia) was able to vote for assemblies that, if not entirely sovereign, did wield significant influence. In the Italian case the advance was particularly striking, for, with the triumph of the *Risorgimento*, the Piedmontese constitution was applied to territories that had previously been ruled by some of the most arbitrary governments in Europe.[1] And in France, despite the humiliations attending the birth of the Third Republic, democracy came through unscathed. The mood that sought expiation in a return to the good old ways of the past – even a restoration of the monarchy – soon began to ebb. It left behind a suitably vacuous monument in the form of the Sacré Coeur (built on the site of the gun park where the 1871 insurrection had begun), but it left intact the Republic and the republican tradition of universal male suffrage.

In the economic sphere England's dominance remained almost as complete as it had been a generation earlier. The British Isles still produced 60 per cent of Europe's coal and iron, much the same proportion as it had in 1848. If other countries were catching up as far as railways were concerned, this was more to do with their size than a closing of the technological gap: Germany, now poised to overtake Britain in terms of mileage of track, obviously needed a bigger network than the United Kingdom. Even here the comparison is more in Britain's favour than the raw figures suggest, for whereas Britain's railways were built by her entrepreneurs, the expansion of the German railway system was partly financed by the military.[2]

1. *Il Risorgimento* ('The Resurgence') is the name Cavour chose for the newspaper he founded in 1848 to promote the cause of Italian unity; historians have adopted it as a convenient label for the movement as a whole.
2. Moltke always refused funds for fortresses, saying the money was better spent on railways. This wasn't just a *bon mot*: meticulously worked out railway mobilization schedules were the cornerstone of his strategic planning – and the reason why the German army got off to such a good start in both 1866 and 1870.

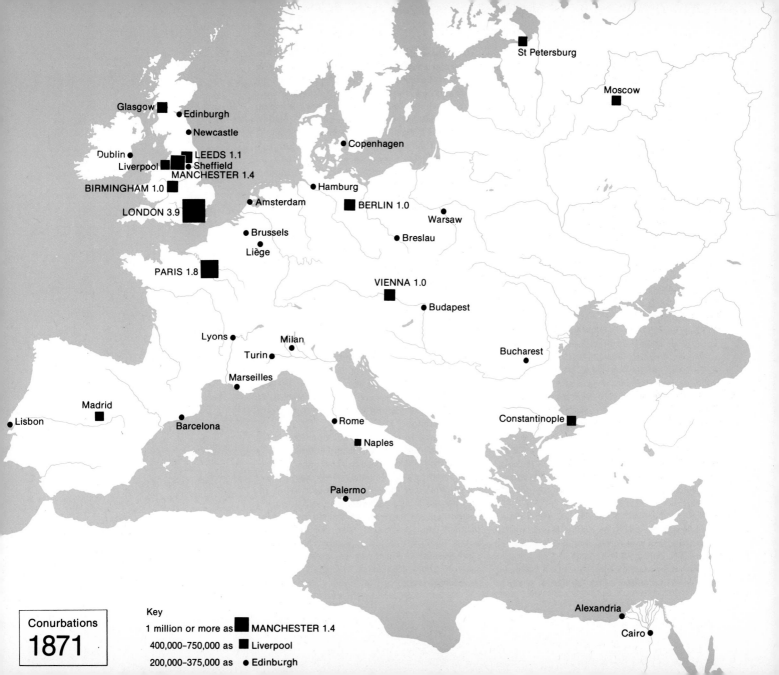

Glasgow

Edinburgh

Newcastle

St Petersburg

Moscow

Copenhagen

Dublin

LEEDS 1.1

Liverpool Sheffield

MANCHESTER 1.4

BIRMINGHAM 1.0

Hamburg

Amsterdam

BERLIN 1.0

Warsaw

LONDON 3.9

Breslau

Brussels

Liège

PARIS 1.8

VIENNA 1.0

Budapest

Lyons

Milan

Bucharest

Turin

Marseilles

Madrid

Rome

Constantinople

Lisbon

Barcelona

Naples

Palermo

Alexandria

Cairo

Conurbations
1871

Key

1 million or more as ■ MANCHESTER 1.4

400,000–750,000 as ■ Liverpool

200,000–375,000 as ● Edinburgh

BETWEEN 1848 AND 1871 the population of the Russian Empire grew by twenty millions, or more than a quarter; this was a rate of increase that only Britain could match and, because of the loss of population in Ireland, the overall figure of the United Kingdom was considerably lower, only 15 per cent. As Russia had started off with a bigger population than any other European power, her preponderance was increased: she now had more than twice as many people as the next in line, the German Empire with its forty-one millions. Pushed down to equal third (from equal second) were France and the Austro-Hungarian Empire: neither showed any gain on their 1848 figures because their territorial losses (Alsace-Lorraine in the case of France, Lombardy and Venetia in the case of Austria-Hungary) cancelled out their natural increase. The United Kingdom now came close behind these two; in sixth place was the new Kingdom of Italy, then Spain.

These population rankings had special significance to the politicians of the generation following the Franco-Prussian War. The war had shown that a large conscript army was a much better bet than a small professional one; if an island kingdom like Britain, whose defence needs were largely met by the Royal Navy, could afford to ignore the lesson, the continental nations couldn't and didn't: within a few years all of them had passed laws making military service compulsory. Manpower had become a key resource and from now on generals went for census returns like schoolboys after comics: in the cohorts of the demographer they saw the army corps of the future.

The introduction of conscription had some interesting effects on military ratings. Russia, written down since the Crimean War, began to be written up again: not only could she mobilize an immense number of men, but, now that she had a reasonable railway network, she could, in theory, begin to deploy them effectively. On the other hand the German generals found half their advantage gone. Moltke reckoned there was little chance of winning quick victories in another war with France because there would be so many French divisions drawn up along the new and shorter frontier that it would be impossible to fight one's way through them. It followed from this that in a general European conflict Germany's best strategy would be to stand on the defensive in the west and go for a quick decision in the east. When Moltke retired in 1888, this analysis formed the basis of the plans he bequeathed his successor.

Note that the Habsburg Empire is now no longer Austrian, but Austro-Hungarian. In 1867 the Emperor Franz Joseph, recognizing that something had to be done to strengthen his regime following the defeats of 1859 and, more particularly, 1866, decided to take the Hungarians into partnership. He gave them not just autonomy but control of the Slav peoples living within the ancient boundaries of the Hungarian kingdom: the Slovaks of the Carpathians in the north, the Serbs of the frontier zone in the south and the Croats, who had once had their own sub-kingdom, in the south-west. Because the new constitution stressed the distinction between Franz Joseph's Austrian and Hungarian dominions, this refurbished empire is often referred to as the Dual Monarchy.

Like Franz Joseph, the Dual Monarchy lasted longer than anyone expected. This was partly because the Habsburgs had lost their most troublesome minority, the Italians, partly because the Hungarians were every bit as ruthless about repressing the subject minorities as the Austrians – some would say more so – and partly because the national consciousness of these minorities (very largely Slav) was only just awakening. Nonetheless, a polyglot state of this sort was now an obvious anomaly and anomalies are dangerous things to leave lying around.

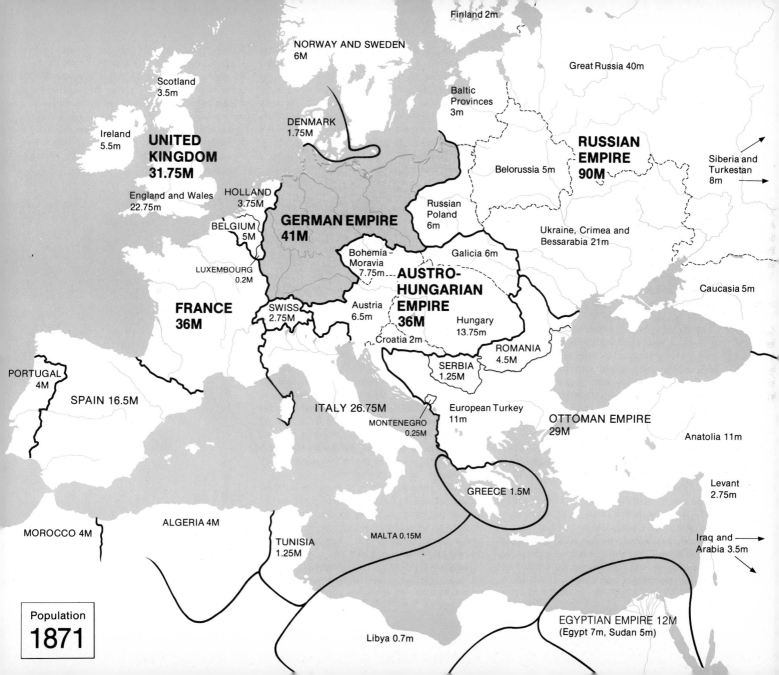

Finland 2m

NORWAY AND SWEDEN
6M

Great Russia 40m

Scotland
3.5m

Baltic
Provinces
3m

Ireland
5.5m

UNITED
KINGDOM
31.75M

DENMARK
1.75M

RUSSIAN
EMPIRE
90M

Siberia and
Turkestan
8m

England and Wales
22.75m

HOLLAND
3.75M

Belorussia 5m

BELGIUM
5M

GERMAN EMPIRE
41M

Russian
Poland
6m

Ukraine, Crimea and
Bessarabia 21m

LUXEMBOURG
0.2M

Galicia 6m

Bohemia-
Moravia
7.75m

AUSTRO-
HUNGARIAN
EMPIRE
36M

Caucasia 5m

FRANCE
36M

SWISS
2.75M

Austria
6.5m

Hungary
13.75m

PORTUGAL
4M

Croatia 2m

ROMANIA
4.5M

SPAIN 16.5M

SERBIA
1.25M

ITALY 26.75M

MONTENEGRO
0.25M

European Turkey
11m

OTTOMAN EMPIRE
29M

Anatolia 11m

GREECE 1.5M

Levant
2.75m

MOROCCO 4M

ALGERIA 4M

TUNISIA
1.25M

MALTA 0.15M

Iraq and
Arabia 3.5m

Population
1871

Libya 0.7m

EGYPTIAN EMPIRE 12M
(Egypt 7m, Sudan 5m)

ON THE OUTBREAK of the Franco-Prussian War Napoleon III recalled the French garrison from Rome. For years he had been looking for a graceful way of liquidating his commitment to the Papacy; now military necessity gave him the excuse he needed. The French army marched out, the Italian army marched in, the Eternal City became the capital of the Italian kingdom (an office that Florence had filled in the interim) and the Papal administration was confined to the Vatican and a few other buildings in or near Rome.

France's difficulties opened up political opportunities for other countries besides Italy – in particular for Russia, where the terms imposed by the French and British at the end of the Crimean War were still bitterly resented. The Russians acted very cautiously, though. Their first move was simply to declare their intention of building up a Black Sea fleet again, something they had been made to promise not to, but which, as Bismarck remarked, no one could stop them doing if they really wanted to. Even so, when the British protested they agreed to turn their declaration into a 'proposal' and have it discussed at an international conference (in London, in 1871); needless to say, it was accepted. And with this, for the moment, they remained content. Not till 1877 did they challenge the essential prohibition of the Crimean treaty, which can be summed up as 'Hands off Turkey', and they only did so then because public opinion in Europe had swung in their favour – indeed was positively demanding that Russian troops rescue the Balkan Christians from the Terrible Turk.

This turn of events had begun in 1875 with a rising by the Bosnians against Turkish rule. Bosnia was a long way from Constantinople, further than the Sultan's failing military powers could easily reach, and the Bosnian rebels scored success after success. This encouraged the Bulgars to try their luck. Their case was very different: the Turks were still able to stamp on people as close to home as this and they proceeded to do so with vicious efficiency. As news of the massacres leaked out, public opinion in Europe was aroused; everyone cheered on the Serbs as they hurried to the rescue. Alas, the Turks easily defeated the Serbs and it was clear that if the Bulgars were going to be rescued at all it could only be by Big Brother Russia. Hence the general agreement among the Powers that the Tsar could send an army south of the Danube.

The expeditionary force that the Tsar dispatched arrived at the Turkish frontier in April 1877; its commanders were so confident that the campaign was going to be a walk-over that they refused a Romanian offer of help. However, they had only got to Plevna, some twenty-five miles south of the Danube, when they were rebuffed by a Turkish division commanded by Osman Pasha. By digging in and hanging on, Osman held up the whole Russian army for five months. It was long enough for public opinion in Europe to swing back in favour of the Gallant Turk. When the Russians finally reached the gates of Constantinople (in January 1878), they were able to make the Sultan sign away his Balkan provinces, but they no longer had the approval of the Powers for their action. Indeed, the British, who had sent their fleet to Constantinople, made it quite clear they weren't prepared to accept the new treaty at all. A dispirited Tsar took up Bismarck's offer to act as 'an honest broker' and everyone met in Berlin in 1878 under the chairmanship of the new – and, in this instance, relatively disinterested – arbiter of Europe.

Britain's opposition really worried the Russians because, despite the fuss they made about their right to keep battleships in the Black Sea, they hadn't actually got around to building any. Rather than face a second Crimean War, they backed down, dropping the idea of a big Bulgaria – it was to have covered two-thirds of the Turkish territory south of the lower Danube – and settling instead for a Bulgaria that was half the size, divided in two (Bulgaria and East Rumelia) and had restrictions on its autonomy. A grateful Sultan gave the British permission to occupy Cyprus, the Austrians got Bosnia (which the Russians had promised them at the start of the war) on similar terms and Romania, Serbia and Montenegro were each enlarged a bit. All Russia gained was the restoration of the slice of Bessarabia it had lost in 1856, plus a few towns in Caucasia (off the map).

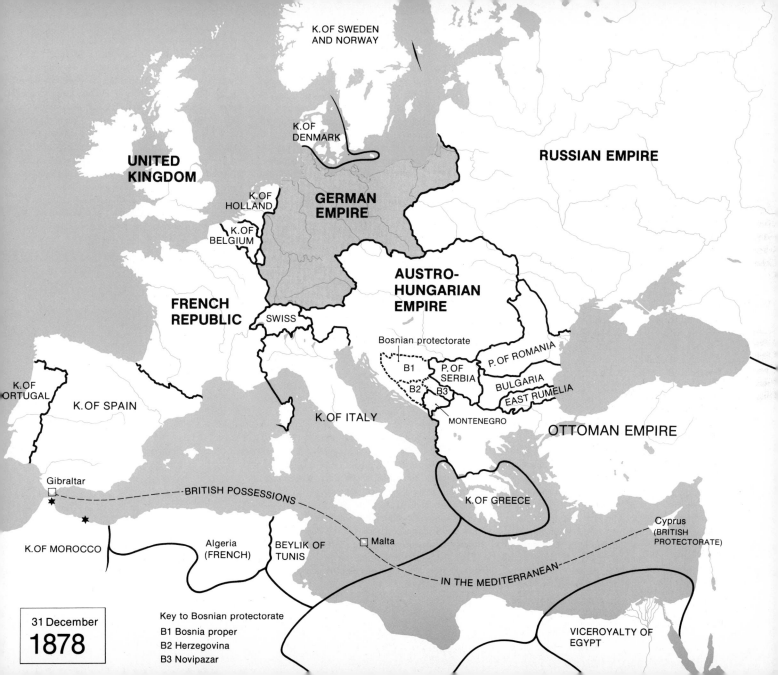

K.OF SWEDEN
AND NORWAY

RUSSIAN EMPIRE

K.OF
DENMARK

UNITED
KINGDOM

K.OF
HOLLAND

GERMAN
EMPIRE

K.OF
BELGIUM

FRENCH
REPUBLIC

AUSTRO-
HUNGARIAN
EMPIRE

SWISS

Bosnian protectorate

P. OF ROMANIA

B1

P. OF
SERBIA

K.OF
PORTUGAL

K.OF SPAIN

B2

B3

BULGARIA

K.OF ITALY

EAST RUMELIA

MONTENEGRO

OTTOMAN EMPIRE

Gibraltar

BRITISH POSSESSIONS

K.OF GREECE

Cyprus
(BRITISH
PROTECTORATE)

K.OF MOROCCO

Algeria
(FRENCH)

BEYLIK OF
TUNIS

Malta

IN THE MEDITERRANEAN

VICEROYALTY OF
EGYPT

31 December
1878

Key to Bosnian protectorate
B1 Bosnia proper
B2 Herzegovina
B3 Novipazar

THE CONGRESS OF BERLIN broke up before it had finished all its business. There was the question of Tunis, which had been offered to the French because everyone – even the Germans – felt sorry for them; the French were still hovering as to whether to accept it or not. And then, what about the Greeks? There was a general feeling that the time had come to give them a bit more of their homeland, but exactly how much was still being discussed. In fact it wasn't till 1881 that the final settlements were made, with the French taking Tunis – they did so more to forestall the Italians than because they wanted it themselves – and the Greeks getting Thessaly.

France's interest in North Africa was not limited to the Maghreb (the western sector: present-day Morocco, Algeria and Tunisia); she also had important emotional and commercial commitments in Egypt. Ever since Napoleon Bonaparte's expedition there in 1798, Frenchmen had felt that it was their destiny to help this ancient country find a place in the modern world; if anyone wanted an example of what this meant in practical terms, what better example could they have than the Suez Canal? Conceived and executed by the French engineer de Lesseps, financed almost entirely by French capital, the canal had been opened (in 1869) in a ceremony conducted jointly by Napoleon III and the Egyptian ruler, Khedive Ismail (Mohammed Ali's grandson). By 1875 it was on the verge of profitability. But here was the rub. The profligate Ismail had run Egypt's foreign debt up so high and his creditors were dunning him so hard that he couldn't wait for his dividends – he had to have money right away. Reluctantly, he placed his last asset, his 44 per cent share in the Suez Canal Company, on the market. Recognizing the opportunity, Disraeli, now Britain's Prime Minister, bought the entire holding, so transforming what had been a Franco-Egyptian company into a British-dominated one. This was

bad enough for French pride, but worse was to follow. The £4 million the Khedive received for his shares only lasted him a year and in 1879 his French and British bankers agreed that they would have to put their own financial officials in charge of the Egyptian treasury if the rot was ever to be stopped. Inevitably there was a fierce nationalist reaction to this measure, with anti-foreign riots which the Egyptian government proved unable or unwilling to control. This activated the imperial reflex. The British fleet arrived, then the British army, and in the course of 1882 the entire country was brought under British control.

The French were furious. Through lack of resources they had had to turn down the British offer of joint action and they quite clearly lacked the muscle to do anything about it at this late stage. But to see Egypt, which they had wooed so long and so carefully, bundled unceremoniously into the British Empire was almost more than they could bear. Bismarck must have smiled as he watched the French give free rein to their anglophobia – and perpetuate their isolation.

Bismarck's new order was now almost impregnable: all he had to do was stop the French making friends. It was the simplest possible prescription for peace, and peace was about to descend on Europe for a generation. Before it did so, however, there was to be one more scuffle in the Balkans, the Bulgar-Serb War of 1885. This was precipitated by the Bulgars announcing, in defiance of the Berlin settlement, the union of East Rumelia and Bulgaria; the Serbs, prodded by Austria (both wanted a weak Bulgaria), immediately challenged them but met military defeat. Such were the convolutions of contemporary diplomacy that it was now the British who supported the Bulgarians and the Russians who upheld the sanctity of the Berlin terms. Eventually common sense prevailed and the Bulgars were allowed to bring the two halves of their country together.

Bismarck presided over the Empire he had created for a further five years; then a new Emperor, the bombastic little Wilhelm II, dismissed him from the Chancellorship. A hero in his own time, he has had a bad press since, partly because he could never pass up an opportunity to outrage liberal opinion ('The issues of our day will not be decided by the ballot box, but by blood and iron'), partly because, by his very success, he stunted the hitherto rather promising growth of democratic institutions in Germany. But, though he was a reactionary, he was not a fanatic and the way German nationalism developed over the next generation wouldn't have appealed to him at all. He always knew when to stop.

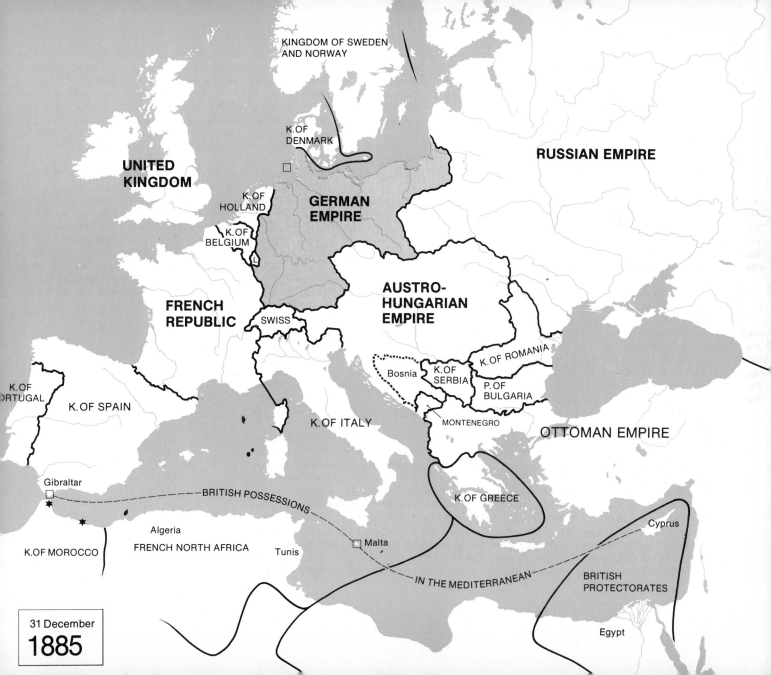

KINGDOM OF SWEDEN
AND NORWAY

RUSSIAN EMPIRE

K.OF
DENMARK

UNITED
KINGDOM

K.OF
HOLLAND

GERMAN
EMPIRE

K.OF
BELGIUM

L

FRENCH
REPUBLIC

AUSTRO-
HUNGARIAN
EMPIRE

SWISS

K.OF
PORTUGAL

Bosnia

K.OF ROMANIA

K.OF
SERBIA

P. OF
BULGARIA

K.OF SPAIN

K.OF ITALY

MONTENEGRO

OTTOMAN EMPIRE

Gibraltar

BRITISH POSSESSIONS

K.OF GREECE

Cyprus

Algeria

K.OF MOROCCO

FRENCH NORTH AFRICA

Tunis

Malta

IN THE MEDITERRANEAN

BRITISH
PROTECTORATES

Egypt

31 December
1885

BETWEEN 1885 AND 1910 – a period of twenty-five years – there were no wars in Europe and almost no boundary changes. Well, to be truthful, there was a small war between Greece and Turkey in 1897 (which resulted in adjustments, invisible on a map of this scale, to the frontier in Thessaly) and some revolts in Crete, which led to that island being given an internationally supervised autonomy (1898) as a preliminary to its annexation by Greece (which took place in 1912). But otherwise there was complete peace and quiet and the few territorial changes that took place were a matter of agreement or proclamation. The British, realizing that Heligoland was no use to them any more – advances in naval technology made it, and the whole concept of close blockade, untenable – ceded it to Germany in exchange for Zanzibar (1890). The Norwegians declared their union with Sweden at an end in 1905; after marching into the country – something the Norwegians made no attempt to prevent – the Swedes decided to let them have their way and marched out again. And in 1908 the Austro-Hungarians annexed the major part of their Bosnian protectorate (Bosnia proper and Herzegovina), while withdrawing from the remainder (Novipazar). The only other change was purely dynastic, the dissolution of the personal link between the Kingdom of Holland and the Duchy of Luxembourg on the accession of Holland's Queen Wilhemina in 1890, since the Duchy's inheritance laws excluded females.

But if the political map of Europe stayed the same, the realities underlying it changed a great deal. Most important was the way the German Empire had moved into a class of its own. Bismarck had made Germany the strongest of the continental powers; the German Empire of the turn of the century was stronger than any other two. This was bad all round. It made the Germans arrogant, and overly suscept-

ible to the sort of master-race theories which all European nations inclined to at this time. And it pushed France and Russia, the two powers with most to fear from German bullying, into a defensive alliance. Paradoxically – because it brought the military equation nearer balance – this increased the risk of war. What was really alarming was that the Germans didn't see any of this. The Franco-Russian alliance, which Bismarck would have given top priority to undoing, caused very little concern either when it was first effected (in 1892) or subsequently; the German army was considered perfectly capable of taking on the Frogs and Russkies at the same time and teaching them both a lesson. And the British too.

Adding Britain to the list of Germany's enemies was the personal achievement of the Emperor Wilhelm II. An addicted sabre-rattler, he announced that he was going to take the Boer state of Transvaal under his protection just when the British had finally made up their minds to annex it (1897). They were understandably furious and, when he discovered that because he hadn't got a fleet he couldn't make his protection effective, so was he. He threw his influence behind a naval construction programme designed to give Germany a world-class fleet within twenty years; this policy, for which there was no shortage of popular support, ensured that the breach with Britain became permanent.

Just how far ahead of themselves the Germans were getting soon became apparent. In 1905 the French were putting the finishing touches to a plan they had for taking over Morocco: they had settled their differences with the other interested powers – the British (by recognizing their position in Egypt), the Italians (by promising them a free hand in Libya) and the Spanish (by making them partners) – and were just about to move in when Wilhelm made another of his special contributions. Landing at Tangier, he declared that Germany regarded

Morocco as a fully independent state. France would have to back down, a ceremony to be performed in public at an international conference.

France did no such thing. Egged on by the British, the French stood firm and it was the Germans – who had the support of no one except Austria-Hungary – who had to change their position. France's 'special interest' in Morocco was recognized by the international community and all Wilhelm got for his trouble was a bit of Central Africa too small to cover his loss of face.

This diplomatic debacle should have been a warning to Germany's super-patriots, but it acted as a spur instead. The naval programme was accelerated. Russia was threatened, not conciliated, when she protested at Austria-Hungary's annexation of Bosnia. And Austria-Hungary was encouraged to think that if she pursued a forward policy in the Balkans she could count on German backing.

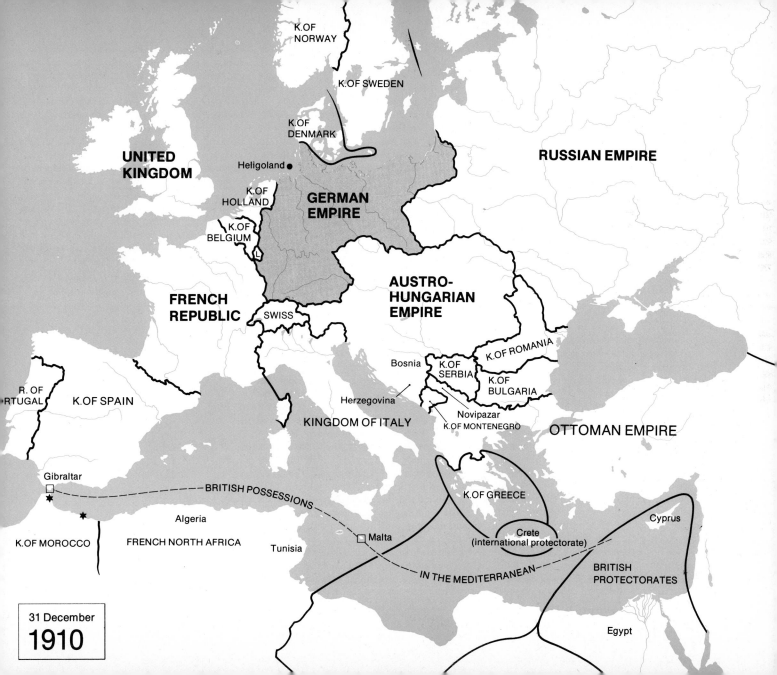

K.OF
NORWAY

K.OF SWEDEN

K.OF
DENMARK

**UNITED
KINGDOM**

Heligoland ●

RUSSIAN EMPIRE

K.OF
HOLLAND

**GERMAN
EMPIRE**

K.OF
BELGIUM

L

**FRENCH
REPUBLIC**

SWISS

**AUSTRO-
HUNGARIAN
EMPIRE**

R. OF
RTUGAL

K.OF SPAIN

Bosnia

K.OF ROMANIA

K.OF SERBIA

Herzegovina

K.OF
BULGARIA

KINGDOM OF ITALY

Novipazar
K.OF MONTENEGRO

OTTOMAN EMPIRE

Gibraltar
□
★

— — BRITISH POSSESSIONS

K.OF GREECE

Cyprus

★

Algeria

K.OF MOROCCO

FRENCH NORTH AFRICA

Tunisia

□ Malta

Crete
(international protectorate)

**BRITISH
PROTECTORATES**

IN THE MEDITERRANEAN

Egypt

31 December
1910

IN THE CLOSING DECADES of the nineteenth century the German Empire displaced the United Kingdom from its traditional position as Europe's leading industrial power. By 1910, though Britain was still ahead in coal mining, textiles and shipping, Germany had a comfortable lead in iron and steel production and was way out in front when it came to the new technologies – electrical, chemical and mechanical.

Nothing signals Germany's new status more clearly than the growth of its cities. In 1871 only three places in the whole of the Empire rated a place on the map; between them they contained a bare 4 per cent of the population. By 1910 the number of towns qualifying has risen to twenty-five and the proportion of the (much larger) population living in them has jumped to a quarter. Britain might still have a bigger urban population (just) and a considerably higher urban proportion (over 40 per cent), but she couldn't match Germany's growth rate. Particularly noteworthy in this context is the Ruhr conurbation: the big towns at the heart of this – Essen, Dortmund, Duisburg and Bochum – had been villages a generation earlier; now they constituted the most powerful productive unit in Europe.

Trailing way behind Germany and Britain were the other three major powers: France, Austria-Hungary and Russia. Russia was particularly backward: the peasants who constituted more than 80 per cent of its population had lives that were just about as nasty, brutish and short as they had been in the Middle Ages. But even in Russia the industrial revolution had begun to make itself felt and, if the areas affected remained small in proportion to the whole, the scale of everything in Russia is so vast that in aggregate the industrial sector was quite impressive. For example, Russian iron and steel production, though puny in per capita terms, amounted to half Britain's. And though the urban population was only a small fraction of the whole (on the definition used here, a mere 5 per cent) St Petersburg and Moscow were big cities by any standard. Indeed each was as big as Paris had been in the year of the Commune.

Marx had never thought of Russia as a likely venue for the socialist millennium: in evolutionary terms – and Marx was always conscious of Darwinian analogies – it seemed too far behind the rest of Europe for that. But though this was fair enough in his lifetime (1818–83), it had ceased to be a good way of looking at things a generation later. In the advanced countries the material benefits of capitalism were finally beginning to percolate down to the working classes, with the result that the revolutionary impulse was perceptibly slackening; it was the workers in the new industrial cities of Russia whose degradation corresponded best to Marxist theory: they were the ones with nothing to lose but their chains.

This became briefly apparent in 1904–5 when Russia got involved in a disastrous war with Japan. As the arrogance and incompetence of the Tsar's government were revealed for all to see, the exasperation and despair of his subjects found expression in an escalating series of strikes, marches and mutinies. In the countryside the peasants began burning the houses of the gentry; in the towns, workers' councils – 'soviets' – started to issue ultimatums to the local authorities. Even the wooden-headed Tsar perceived the need for concessions and reluctantly and insincerely agreed to the grant of an 1848-style liberal constitution. This did the trick. The people began to drift back to work, the troops returned to their loyalties and the government recovered the initiative. At the end of the year the authorities felt strong enough to order the arrest of the workers' councils. The St Petersburg Soviet went quietly; the Moscow Soviet, which was dominated by hard-line Communists, tried to fight it out, but the few squads of armed workers it could call on were soon shot down. By the end of 1906 it was all over: the strikes were broken, the constitution had been emasculated and the Tsar was ruling as autocratically as ever.

As the Russo-Japanese War indicates, Europe was no longer making all the running: key events could be triggered off by non-European powers. And one of the most important events of the era had nothing to do with Europe at all. For Germany had not been the first nation to overtake Britain industrially; that had been done by the United States back in the early 1880s. Since then, further growth had taken the USA into a class of its own: by 1910 it was producing more iron and steel than Britain and Germany put together; it was also producing more coal than either and two-thirds of the world's supply of oil, the fuel of the future, of which neither Britain nor Germany had any at all. The New World had spawned the first superpower.

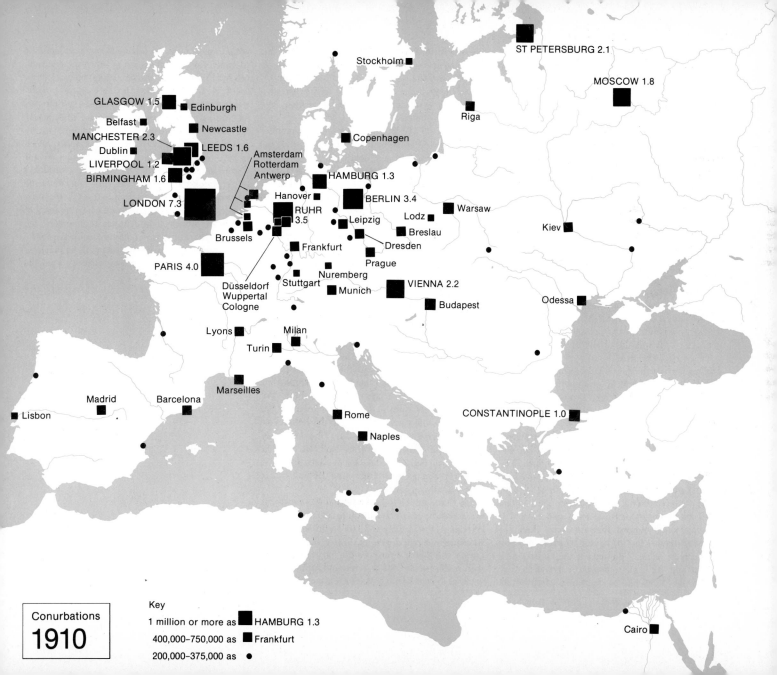

ST PETERSBURG 2.1

MOSCOW 1.8

Stockholm

Riga

GLASGOW 1.5   Edinburgh

Belfast   Newcastle

MANCHESTER 2.3   Copenhagen

Dublin   LEEDS 1.6

LIVERPOOL 1.2   Amsterdam
Rotterdam
BIRMINGHAM 1.6   Antwerp

Hanover   HAMBURG 1.3   BERLIN 3.4   Warsaw

LONDON 7.3   RUHR   Leipzig   Lodz
3.5   Breslau   Kiev

Brussels   Dresden

Frankfurt   Prague

PARIS 4.0   Nuremberg   Odessa

Düsseldorf   Stuttgart   VIENNA 2.2
Wuppertal   Munich
Cologne   Budapest

Lyons   Milan

Turin

Marseilles

Lisbon   Madrid   Barcelona   CONSTANTINOPLE 1.0

Rome

Naples

Cairo

Conurbations
1910

Key

1 million or more as ■ HAMBURG 1.3

400,000–750,000 as ■ Frankfurt

200,000–375,000 as ●

EUROPE'S POPULATION increased by nearly 50 per cent in the period 1871–1910, faster than ever before or since. The biggest gains, both absolutely and proportionately, were registered by the biggest powers: Russia put on eighty millions (an 88 per cent increase) and Germany twenty millions (60 per cent). Britain's increase would have been in much the same proportion as Germany's, if it hadn't been for Ireland, which was still losing people; as it was, the United Kingdom only managed a 40 per cent gain. This was still enough to give it, for the first time, a bigger population than France. The French performance was truly lamentable: a 10 per cent increment, the lowest in Europe. Of the five major powers, France now ranked fifth in population terms; it had slipped three places in the course of a century.[1]

Austria-Hungary's increase was 33 per cent, a perfectly respectable figure that kept the Habsburgs well up among the Great Powers. But the Empire's demographic problem was not and never had been quantitative; it was the totally intractable one of heterogeneity. And here things were getting worse. The proportion of Slavs was approaching 50 per cent and this, taken in conjunction with the increasing political awareness shown by many of them, was bringing the Empire to another crisis of identity.

Not that the Slavs didn't have identity problems too: despite a lot of talk about pan-Slavism, the world of the Slavs was far from being united. The Slavs of the Balkans were geographically separated from the Slavs of eastern Europe; there was an equally deep emotional divide between the Catholic Poles and the Orthodox Russians. A glance at a map like this might suggest that the main threat to Austria-Hungary lay in the north, where the Slav superpower, Russia, abutted on the entirely Slav (Polish and Ruthenian) province of Galicia. Far from it. The Poles had no interest in a Polish state unless it was a free and independent one, nor the Ruthenians (Ukrainians) any wish to join a Ukraine that was less than autonomous. If staying put or joining the Russians was the choice, they would stay where they were. Franz Joseph never had any trouble with Galicia.

The Slavs of the Balkans were another matter. Though the different peoples there had separate identities, these had not developed so far as to exclude the idea of a single Yugoslav (south Slav) state. The idea appealed least to the peoples at either end of the geographical distribution: the Croats (who were Catholic and regarded themselves as Western Europeans) and the Bulgars (who already had a state of their own). Conversely, it was the people in the middle, the Serbs, who were Yugoslavia's most enthusiastic proponents. They spread the gospel among their immediate neighbours, the Montenegrans and Bosnians, with great fervour and considerable success.

It was to put a stop to the pro-Serb drift in Bosnia that the Austrians annexed the province in 1908. This was an illegal act – the 1878 treaty gave them occupation rights only – and the Serbs were justly outraged. They appealed to the Russians in the name of pan-Slavism and the Russians protested to the Germans and Austrians in the name of the 1878 treaty. But Russia was in no condition to fight – the country was still convalescing from the 1905 revolution – and the Germans knew it. They brusquely rejected the Russian protests and encouraged Austria to do the same. The Russians had to swallow their pride and tell themselves – and the Serbs – that there was always another day.

For Franz Joseph to annex Bosnia was one thing; to reconcile its people to Habsburg rule was another. Perhaps it was already too late to do so, but one Habsburg was prepared to have a try, the heir to the throne, Archduke Franz Ferdinand. He let it be known that he favoured a reorganization of the imperial system so that the Slavs got more of the good things of life. According to some, he intended to transform the dual monarchy into a tripartite one (an equal alliance of Austrian, Hungarian and Slav); according to others – and this view seems more likely – he was thinking in terms of making the Empire a federation of states, some of which would be purely Slav. What is certain is that his ideas didn't find any favour with the Emperor Franz Joseph, as indeed none of his ideas had since his marriage to a lady (of Czech descent) whom the Emperor considered unsuitable. But though the Emperor could make life uncomfortable for the lady in question (she was only allowed to call herself a duchess, which meant that all the Habsburg archduchesses took precedence over her), he couldn't alter the succession. And as he was now eighty years old, it couldn't be all that long before Franz Ferdinand got his chance to put the Empire on a new course.

1. The figures for Europe given in this section are exclusive of Siberia and Russian Turkestan; the figures for the Russian Empire include both.

NORWAY 2.5M

Finland 3m

Great Russia 70m

SWEDEN 5.5M

Scotland 4.5m

Baltic Provinces 4.5m

RUSSIAN EMPIRE 170M

Siberia and Turkestan 22m

Ireland 4.5m

UNITED KINGDOM 45M

DENMARK 2.75M

Belorussia 10m

HOLLAND 6M

England and Wales 36m

Russian Poland 12.5m

Ukraine, Crimea and Bessarabia 39m

BELGIUM 7.5M

GERMAN EMPIRE 65M

Bohemia Moravia 9.25m

Galicia 8.75m

LUXEMBOURG 0.25M

AUSTRO-HUNGARIAN EMPIRE 50M

Caucasia 9m

FRANCE 39.5M

SWISS 3.75M

Austria 9m

Hungary 18m

PORTUGAL 5.5M

Croatia 3m

ROMANIA 7M

SPAIN 19M

Bosnia 2m

SERBIA 3M

BULGARIA 4.25M

ITALY 34.5M

MONTENEGRO 0.5M

European Turkey 6m

OTTOMAN EMPIRE 27M

Anatolia 13m

GREECE 3M

CYPRUS 0.25M

Levant 3m

ALGERIA 5.25M

TUNISIA 1.5M

MALTA 0.2M

MOROCCO 5.25M

Iraq and Arabia 4.25m

Libya 0.75m

EGYPT 11M

Population 1910

SLAVS

IN MARCH 1912 the French finally moved into Morocco, establishing a formal protectorate over the country. Spain got her share, as arranged, and this time Germany was paid off too, with a slice of the French Congo. Italy was already in the process of picking up her sweetener, Libya.

None of these moves went entirely smoothly. It took the French and Spanish armies many years of hard fighting to reduce the tribesmen of the Moroccan Atlas, and the Italians, after a misleadingly easy start, were to have even more trouble with the Bedouin of the Libyan hinterland. Even getting the Turks to sign over the province gave the Italians problems: it wasn't till the Italian navy entered the Aegean and occupied Rhodes and the neighbouring islands (twelve in all, hence the term Dodecanese) that the Turks would agree to a formal peace; even then they did so more because of the outbreak of the First Balkan War than because they were frightened of the Italians.

The First Balkan War (October 1912 to May 1913) turned out disastrously for Turkey. The Serbs, Greeks and Bulgars had come to the conclusion that if they all acted together they were strong enough to dismember Turkey-in-Europe. Events quickly proved them right. Within a month the Bulgars had reached the gates of Constantinople (though they were repulsed when they got there), the Serbs had taken Skopje and the Greeks were closing in on Salonika. By December 1912 there was nothing the Turks could do but ask for a truce. There was another round of fighting in early 1913, but this merely served to confirm the original result. Turkey's only hope was that its enemies would fall out.

This they did remarkably quickly. The Bulgars, angry because they had fought the hardest and gained the least, quietly switched their army from east to west and fell on the Serbs and Greeks. Their treachery served them ill: they were quickly beaten back to their own lines and, while their forces were committed to this unsuccessful foray, the Turks were able to launch an offensive that recovered Adrianople. The Bulgars also lost the southern Dobruja to a Romanian invasion. The frontiers agreed at the end of this, the Second Balkan War (June to July 1913), pictured Bulgaria's humiliation as much as Turkey's. Serbia and Greece emerged 50 per cent bigger (and with populations increased in proportion, from three millions to four and a half millions apiece); Bulgaria's losses nearly cancelled out her gains.

The peace treaties that put an end to the Balkan Wars brought a new kingdom, Albania, into the European community. The million or so Albanians were mostly Muslim and hadn't fought for their freedom or even asked for it: the country owed its existence to Turkey's inability to defend it and Austria's determination that it shouldn't become Serbian. The Austrians insisted that the Albanians were a genuine nationality, nothing to do with the Slavs at all (they were right), and at the international conference that decided the new frontiers they got their way.

Getting the Bosnians to see their future in Habsburg rather than Serbian terms was proving more difficult. The Governor of Bosnia decided to play his trump card and ask Archduke Franz Ferdinand if he would be prepared to tour the province. He could stay at Ilidze, a pleasant little resort a few miles west of the provincial capital Sarajevo, watch the army's summer manoeuvres and chat up the local dignitaries. The Archduke graciously agreed and an itinerary was drawn up by the governor's staff. In early 1914 a copy of this document arrived on the desk of Colonel Dimitrevich, Chief of Serbian Intelligence. This was not the colonel's only job: under the code name Apis, he was the leading figure in the Black Hand, a terrorist organization dedicated to the cause of Yugoslavia. He decided that this cause would be best served by the elimination of the Archduke.

Franz Ferdinand made his ceremonial entry into Sarajevo on 28 June 1914. Stationed at intervals along his route were six members of a Black Hand assassination squad, one of whom lobbed a bomb at the Archduke's car as it passed. The bomb hit the car but bounced off before exploding; the only person it injured was an aide in the car behind. The Archduke sped safely on to the Town Hall and a loyal address, which, by all accounts, he listened to with remarkably good humour. Then, calling for his car again, he set off to visit his aide in hospital. Unfortunately, nobody had told the chauffeur about this and he started out for the museum, the next stop on the official itinerary; Franz Ferdinand had to call a halt while the misunderstanding was straightened out. It never really was. The car had drawn up opposite the fifth member of the assassination squad, a nineteen-year-old student named Gavrilo Princip. He put one bullet into the Archduke and another into the Duchess before taking cyanide himself. The cyanide didn't work, but the bullets did: within twenty minutes both the Archduke and his Duchess were dead.

K.OF
NORWAY

K.OF SWEDEN

K.OF
DENMARK

UNITED
KINGDOM

RUSSIAN EMPIRE

K.OF
HOLLAND

GERMAN
EMPIRE

K.OF
BELGIUM

FRENCH
REPUBLIC

SWISS

AUSTRO-
HUNGARIAN
EMPIRE

K.OF
ROMANIA

R.OF
ORTUGAL

K.OF SPAIN

Sarajevo

K.OF SERBIA

MONTENEGRO

K.OF
BULGARIA

K.OF ITALY

Skopje

Adrianople

K.OF
ALBANIA

Salonika

OTTOMAN EMPIRE

Gibraltar

BRITISH POSSESSIONS

SPANISH

K. OF GREECE

Dodecanese
(ITALIAN)

Cyprus

FRENCH NORTH AFRICA

Malta

BRITISH
PROTECTORATES

IN THE MEDITERRANEAN

Egypt

ITALIAN NORTH AFRICA

28 June
1914

T HE A U S T R I A N S got surprisingly little out of their interrogation of Princip and his fellow conspirators: just the bare fact that the Archduke's assassination had been planned in Belgrade. It was enough. They had decided that this was the moment to crush Serbia and, after making sure that Germany would back them up, they sent the Serbs an ultimatum: 'Let our investigating teams follow up the leads we have in Belgrade – or else.' No sovereign state could accept a demand like this: the Serbs rejected it and Austria mobilized. So did Russia, determined not to let Austria destroy Serbia. So did the Germans, as they had promised the Austrians they would. And at the same time the Germans made sure that France would fight by asking for guarantees of neutrality that the French couldn't possibly give. In the first two weeks of August, while the diplomats were hurrying about delivering formal notice of the start of hostilities, the armies began their deployment – the Central Powers (Germany and Austria-Hungary) had committed themselves to the overthrow of the Franco-Russian entente.

The German army's plan for a two-front war was the work of Count Schlieffen, who had become Chief of the German General Staff when Waldersee, Moltke's successor, retired in 1892. It was clear then that France and Russia were moving closer together and that war with one would almost certainly mean war with both. And the more Count Schlieffen looked at Moltke's plan for this contingency – which boiled down to defence in the west and limited offensives in the east – the less he liked it: a war fought this way could drag on forever. Maybe France and Russia, being basically rural societies, could sustain a long struggle of this type; Germany, with its advanced economy, would quickly be in trouble. What was wanted, indeed what was necessary, was a way of winning the war in a single campaign.

Trying to get a decision in the east was just not on: it simply wasn't possible to knock the Russians out in one go. Nor was the west an easy option. As Moltke had pointed out, now that the French had introduced conscription they would have enough troops at their disposal to man a continuous defence line the length of the Franco-German frontier. An offensive here would have to start off with a series of frontal assaults against prepared positions, not an appetizing prospect for any army, let alone one in a hurry. It was a real dilemma.

Schlieffen's solution was dazzlingly simple. He wasn't going to fight his way through the French; he was going to go round them. His plan called for the entire German army to be deployed in the west, with more than half of it – fifty divisions out of the eighty available – forming up opposite Holland and Belgium. These divisions, constituting the right wing of the army, were to march through Holland and Belgium as fast as they could go, the idea being to reach the Belgian-French frontier within three weeks of mobilization and one week of the start of the march. From there they would sweep through northern France, folding the French army back on itself by overlapping its left. The essence of the plan was to gain space to manoeuvre by marching through the Low Countries; the essence of the manoeuvre was to swing wide enough to catch the whole French army. As Schlieffen said to his corps commanders, 'Let the last man on the right brush the Channel with his sleeve.' Not one French division must escape.

Schlieffen retired in 1906. His successor was Helmuth Moltke, old Moltke's nephew and a bit of a compromiser. He revised the marching orders of the right wing so that Holland could be left undisturbed (but if you are violating the neutrality of one country, why worry about making it two?) and he decided that ten divisions must be kept back to defend the east against the Russians (but what did it matter if some East Prussian farms were burnt so long as the campaign in France ended victoriously?). Schlieffen, hearing of the changes, began to wonder if the new Chief of Staff understood the thinking behind the plan. He sent him memoranda explaining the need to deploy the strongest possible force and was far from reassured by the evasive replies he received. He was still worrying when he died (in 1913): his last words, clearly meant for Moltke, were: 'If nothing else, keep the right wing strong.'

The Germans sent their demand for free passage for their armies to the Belgian government on 2 August 1914. Would the Belgians fight and, if they did, would the British join them? Within a couple of days the Germans knew that the answer to both questions was Yes. They weren't overly concerned about the British because this was going to be a short war and the British army was too small to affect the issue. But the Belgian decision was disappointing: it meant that the fortress complex at Liège, which lay right in the path of the German armies, would have to be taken out. And there were only ten days in which to do it if the Schlieffen movement was to start on time.

The fortifications of Liège itself were obsolete, as everyone knew: General Ludendorff, a protégé of Moltke's, was able to obtain the surrender of the citadel by simply driving up to it and banging on the door! Round the town, however, there was a ring of twelve forts of relatively modern construction and, given the limited time available, these presented a real problem. The Germans put their trust in Krupps of Essen, who had built a special battery of 420mm cannons just for this job. Their trust was not misplaced. The guns took several days to set up but, once in action, needed only a few hours to reduce a fort to rubble. Von Kluck's 1st Army, the force that was to 'brush the Channel with its sleeve', was able to move off on 17 August, almost exactly as scheduled.

(continued overleaf)

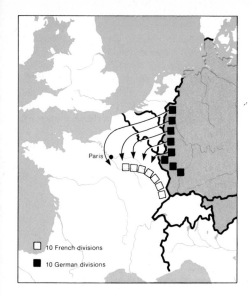

10 French divisions

10 German divisions

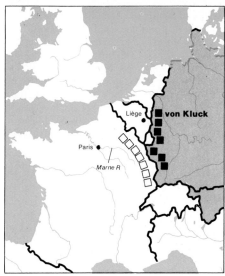

THE SCHLIEFFEN PLAN

August 1914
THE INITIAL DEPLOYMENT

THE WESTERN FRONT IN 1914

A week later von Kluck was on the Franco-Belgian frontier. He had a two to one superiority over the troops the Allies (meaning the French, British and Belgians) had scraped together to stop him and it took him only a day to drive them from their positions. The first phase of the great offensive couldn't have gone better.

The French had an offensive of their own going by this time, a thrust at the German centre. The directive for this, Plan 17, was more a state of mind than an operational document. It proclaimed that all that was needed was to know the enemy's position and attack it, war being just a matter of *cran*, meaning guts. This doctrine, which would have been looked at askance by a Sioux Indian but which had become an article of faith among French military men, soon withered away in the cross-fire of rifle and machine gun. Within a week the French were falling back all along the line, sadder, wiser and fewer.

Meanwhile the Schlieffen Plan unfolded. Von Kluck kept to his schedule by fighting hard and marching harder: by 1 September he was where he was meant to be, at Amiens, fifty miles due north of Paris. But the armies to his left were finding the going stiffer than he was and had had to narrow their fronts to keep up the momentum of their attacks. The German line as a whole was shortening; von Kluck would have to pass east, not west, of Paris.

Von Kluck changed his direction without dropping his pace: on 3 September he crossed the Marne at a point forty miles due east of Paris. It was there that he was hit on the flank by a French force debouching from the capital. It wasn't the attack itself that shook the Germans – von Kluck faced about and beat it off without difficulty; it was the discovery that while they had been shortening their front, the French had been lengthening theirs. By using the railways to transfer whole divisions from right to left the French had built up the forces opposite von Kluck till they outnumbered and

overlapped him. It was immediately clear that the Schlieffen Plan had failed. On Moltke's orders an attempt was made to break through in the centre, but on 9 September the German armies on the right wing began to pull back and re-form. The Allies surged forward, claiming that the 'Battle of the Marne' was a decisive victory. They were quite right, though the victory was entirely in the realm of strategy; there was very little fighting during the turn-around and the Germans consistently had the better of what there was.

The Schlieffen Plan failed for the same reason as Plan 17: the new technology of war – specifically, the vast increase in fire power – had tipped the odds in favour of the defence. For an attack to succeed required more attackers per defender than anyone had foreseen, which is why the Germans had had to shorten their line as they advanced and why the French had been able to lengthen theirs as they retreated. At the time, of course, it was the generalship of the two sides that came under scrutiny, Moltke's 'failure of nerve' being unfavourably contrasted with the complete calm displayed by Joffre, the French Commander. In the case of Joffre the observation was correct, though whether he kept calm because he knew what he was doing (as his admirers believed) or because he never realized how bad things had got (the view taken by his detractors) is a moot point. Certainly Moltke's nerve, or lack of it, didn't influence the result at all. It was the commanders of the armies on the right wing – including von Kluck – who ordered the retreat and they did so as soon as it became clear that it was the German line that was being outflanked; General Headquarters wasn't directly involved.

Blameworthy or not, Moltke was dismissed on 14 September, General Falkenhayn, previously Minister of War, being appointed in his place. Falkenhayn did his best to recover the initiative in the west. As fast as new divisions could be raised, he sent them into northern France with orders to get a new

outflanking movement going. But there was no longer a flank to find: from the Channel to Switzerland the troops stood in continuous array. The fighting became bloodier, but, hard as both sides fought, there was little movement; indeed the battle-line was hardening all the time. By mid-November movement had ceased completely: the troops had dug in and the era of trench warfare had begun.

Army Strengths
Both the French and the Germans brought an extra ten divisions into play during August 1914. The French started out with seventy divisions (disposed much as Schlieffen had anticipated), got a reinforcement of six with the arrival of the British Expeditionary Force and found another four from their own reserves. The additional divisions were added on the left of their line and it was partly due to them that the Allies won the Battle of the Marne. The Germans deployed seventy divisions initially, the eighty Schlieffen had envisaged less the ten Moltke had diverted to the east. Ten extra divisions reached the front during August, but Moltke wasn't able to deploy these where they were needed, on the right wing, because he couldn't get them there on time: they had to be used – and largely wasted – in a direct thrust against the French right.

The French achievement in mobilizing seventy divisions from a population of forty millions – as compared to Germany's eighty divisions from sixty-eight millions – was the basis of their success in 1914. But in the long run they couldn't expect to match Germany's manpower; whereas their army soon levelled off at about 110 divisions, the German went on growing till, in June 1918, it reached a peak strength of 240 divisions. Comparative figures for the other major belligerents are: Russia, 165; the United Kingdom, 90; and Austria-Hungary, 85. The obvious point here is the Russians' failure to make their manpower effective: they were only able to equip and supply a small fraction of the male population available for call-up.

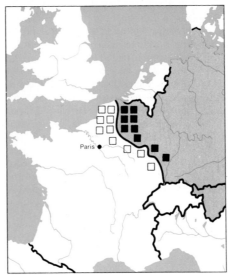

17 August to 3 September 1914
THE MARCH TO THE MARNE

31 December 1914
STALEMATE

THE WESTERN FRONT IN 1914 *(continued)*

WHEN THE GERMANS advanced into Belgium, the Russians, as they had promised the French they would, invaded East Prussia. An army of ten divisions advanced into the province from the east: another of the same size attacked from the south. The first actions went in the Russians' favour and the German commander in Prussia panicked: he telephoned Moltke to say that he was outnumbered two to one and was going to have to retreat. On this occasion none can fault Moltke's response: he immediately ordered Ludendorff to go to Prussia and take over. Ludendorff was a bit on the young side for so important a command (he was just fifty), so Moltke gave him a front man in the ample form of General Hindenburg. Hindenburg, 'the wooden Titan', was sixty-eight years old, tickled pink to be back on the active list and perfectly happy to leave the thinking to Ludendorff. Theirs was to be a memorable partnership.

Ludendorff arrived in the east to find that a plan for a counter-offensive had already been prepared. The basic idea was to concentrate every available unit against the southern Russian army, defeat it, or at least drive it back, and then turn on the eastern one. The snail's-pace advance of the Russians and their use of uncoded radio signals gave Ludendorff the chance to make the initial concentration a really crushing one: at Tannenburg he achieved a classic envelopment and almost completely destroyed the southern Russian force. Then he redeployed against the eastern army and drove it from Prussia with crippling loss. It was a breathtaking feat of arms, something to be set against the failure in the west.[1]

The Austrians, who also had two war fronts, didn't do at all well on either. Their main offensive, a move north from Galicia into Russian Poland, was caught sideways by the Russians' counter-move, a straight drive into Galicia from the east; despite German support the Austrians were unable to recover their balance and by the end of the year all Galicia was in Russian hands. Even worse, the invasion of Serbia, which had been billed as a walk-over, ended in a humiliating rout. The Austrian generals didn't seem to be able to get anything right.

The Germans were understandably bitter about this: the Austrian military had promised a great deal but had turned out to be a complete liability. One German general complained: 'We have shackled ourselves to a corpse.' It was in a way ominous that the traditional 'sick man of Europe', Turkey, was also to be found on the side of the Central Powers, the more so in that the offensives the Turks launched – against the Russians in the Caucasus and the British in Egypt – had the same element of fantasy in them that, in retrospect, it was possible to discern in Austria's pre-war plans.

1. As the map shows, though, the Russians' eastern army recovered quickly enough to make a second drive into East Prussia before the campaigning season was over.

K. OF
NORWAY

K. OF SWEDEN

K. OF
DENMARK

RUSSIAN EMPIRE

**UNITED
KINGDOM**

East
Prussia

Tannenberg ✕

K. OF
HOLLAND

**GERMAN
EMPIRE**

occupied
Belgium

Galicia

**FRENCH
REPUBLIC**

**AUSTRO-
HUNGARIAN
EMPIRE**

SWISS

K. OF
ROMANIA

R. OF
PORTUGAL

K. OF SPAIN

MONTENEGRO

K. OF
SERBIA

K. OF
BULGARIA

OTTOMAN EMPIRE

K. OF ITALY

K. OF
ALBANIA

Gibraltar

SPANISH

BRITISH POSSESSIONS

K. OF GREECE

Dodecanese
(ITALIAN)

Cyprus

FRENCH NORTH AFRICA

Malta

IN THE MEDITERRANEAN

ITALIAN NORTH AFRICA

K. of Egypt
(BRITISH PROTECTORATE)

**31 December
1914**

THE FAILURE of the Schlieffen Plan and of Falkenhayn's attempt to get a revised version going in the closing stages of 1914 left the German High Command without a clear strategy for winning the war. There seemed to be no way of forcing a decisive battle in the west and Falkenhayn, like Schlieffen, was convinced that advances in the east, no matter how dramatic initially, would peter out before a decision could be reached there. But there were enough things that needed to be done – even if they weren't war-winning strokes – to keep Falkenhayn busy through 1915.

First, there was the Austrian sector of the eastern front, which badly needed shoring up. Falkenhayn sent a German army there and in May this force smashed through the Russian line in western Galicia. It then became the southern arm of a vast pincer movement against Russian Poland, the northern arm being provided by Hindenburg and Ludendorff striking south from East Prussia. By early August the Germans were in Warsaw; by early September they were masters of the whole of Russian Poland. Falkenhayn was able to close down the war's first really successful offensive and send the troops south to settle Austria's other little difficulty, Serbia.

Falkenhayn had a new card to play here, for Bulgaria, still smarting from her defeat in the Second Balkan War, had decided to join the Central Powers. This made the conquest of Serbia easy. As the Germans and Austrians opened the main offensive in the north, the Bulgars invaded the south; the whole country was overrun within the month of October. The nucleus of the Serbian army managed a magnificent fighting retreat across the Albanian mountains to the Adriatic and eventual rescue by an Allied naval force, but this hardly seemed important: the Central Powers had the victory and the country.

The Allies, who had seen what was coming in the Balkans, had tried to get help to Serbia by landing a force at Salonika in northern Greece and opening up communications that way. Unfortunately, their expedition was too little and too late and the Bulgars had no difficulty in chasing it back to Salonika; there it continued in uneasy existence, parked on officially neutral territory and serving no visible purpose. Its failure was all the more galling in that adequate forces for a major expedition had been available in the Aegean during the summer but had been squandered on an attempt to take Constantinople. The British navy hadn't been able to force the Dardanelles, so the troops – eventually, a full-scale army ten divisions strong – had been landed outside on the Gallipoli peninsula. There they sat and suffered month after month until finally (in December 1915 and January 1916) the navy took them off again. Such was the power of the machine gun – even in Turkish hands – that the furthest inland any of them had ever got was two miles.[1]

Altogether 1915 was a good year for the Central Powers. The Allied attacks on the western front – where, largely because of the expansion of the British army, and now had a superiority of three to two – had been beaten back with terrible loss (400,000 dead as against a German loss of less than half this number). Serbia had been eliminated. And Russia had been crippled. To some extent these successes were offset by Italy's entry into the war on the Allied side (in May). Italy had cheerfully offered to sell herself to the highest bidder; as the territory she wanted was Austria's, the Allies were understandably prepared to be more generous. But Italy proved a disappointing Ally and her forces never managed to make any impression on the Austrian defence line in the eastern Alps. If the Turks could cope with the British, the Austro-Hungarians could cope with the Italians.

1. One thing the Dardanelles campaign did do was give the Turkish general Mustapha Kemal a chance to show his talents. Starting out as a divisional commander, he ended up the acclaimed 'Saviour of Gallipoli'. It was a success that the Turks badly needed, for their offensive in the Caucasus had ended in total disaster, as had their attempt to seize the Suez Canal.

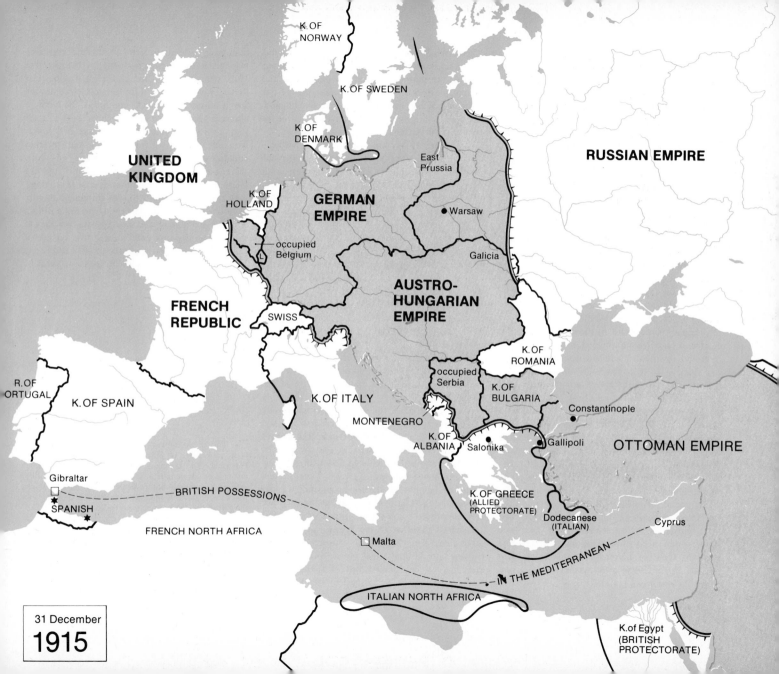

K. OF NORWAY

K. OF SWEDEN

K. OF DENMARK

UNITED KINGDOM

K. OF HOLLAND

East Prussia

RUSSIAN EMPIRE

GERMAN EMPIRE

● Warsaw

occupied Belgium

L

Galicia

FRENCH REPUBLIC

SWISS

AUSTRO-HUNGARIAN EMPIRE

K. OF ROMANIA

R. OF ORTUGAL

K. OF SPAIN

K. OF ITALY

occupied Serbia

K. OF BULGARIA

Constantinople

MONTENEGRO

K. OF ALBANIA

Salonika

Gallipoli

OTTOMAN EMPIRE

Gibraltar

SPANISH

BRITISH POSSESSIONS

K. OF GREECE (ALLIED PROTECTORATE)

Dodecanese (ITALIAN)

Cyprus

FRENCH NORTH AFRICA

☐ Malta

IN THE MEDITERRANEAN

ITALIAN NORTH AFRICA

K. of Egypt (BRITISH PROTECTORATE)

31 December
1915

B Y THE BEGINNING OF 1916 Falken-hayn had tidied up the eastern and Balkan fronts and the crucial problem – how to force a decision in the west – could be put off no longer. Falkenhayn's solution was to attack the French at a point which they felt bound to defend and where he had the tactical advantage, the Verdun salient. He didn't aim to eliminate the salient but just to press it hard enough to draw in the bulk of the French army. And there he would bleed it white. It would be expensive and slow, but the German army should be able to do it.

Falkenhayn began this battle of attrition in May 1916. For the first three months it looked as though his plan might work, then, as the French gradually learnt how to counter the German tactics, the battle deteriorated into a struggle that was just about as punishing for the Germans as the French. Meanwhile the British launched a massive assault in the Somme valley, which reduced this sector of the front to an equally bloody mire. By the end of the year the dead were once again numbered in the hundreds of thousands, but neither side had even the beginnings of a victory. The front line hadn't shifted at all.

In the east, where there were less troops per mile of front and their abilities were more variable, a war of movement was still possible. The Germans could always break through the Russian line if they wanted to and the Russians could punch a hole in the Austro-Hungarian front. In June 1916 Brusilov, the Russian commander in the south, did just that and was rewarded with a progressive collapse of the Austro-Hungarian armies in this sector that pro-duced one of the most spectacular victories of the war. Czech and Slovene units had always performed a bit reluctantly on the Russian front; now they simply threw away their weapons and ran. The Russians took a quarter of a million of them prisoner in the course of an advance that carried across the eastern half of Galicia.

Brusilov's drive then petered out, but before it did so, it had an important political result: Romania decided to throw in its lot with the entente. Like the Italians, the Romanians hoped to win territory from Austria-Hungary; unfortunately, like the Italians, they were militarily so inept that they proved as much of a burden as a help to the Allied cause.

The failure at Verdun had weakened Falken-hayn's position; after the Brusilov offensive he had to resign. Ludendorff, trundling Hindenburg along with him, became the new number one. He quickly re-established the situation in the east, stiffening the Austro-Hungarian units with German officers and NCOs. Then he sent enough troops to Hungary and Bulgaria to spearhead an offensive against Romania. Given Romania's geography, it was easy to arrange for converging attacks that cut off the southern two-thirds of the country. The end of the year saw the shattered remnants of the Romanian army hiding behind a Russian relief force in Moldavia, while the Germans methodically drained the conquered part of the country of its cattle, wheat and oil.

Welcome though this new source of supply was, it wasn't enough. At the beginning of the war the British had established a naval blockade of the Central Powers which, by 1916, was really beginning to hurt. The queues for food in Germany were getting longer and their behaviour less orderly; indeed, in several of the major industrial centres there had been serious riots in the spring. The situation was even worse in Austria-Hungary. The need for that war-winning idea was now really acute.

Surprisingly enough, the best proposition was put forward by the German navy. Germany's surface fleet had proved a non-starter, quite unable to offer a sustained challenge to the British navy, but the submarine arm had done surprisingly well. However, for U-boat attacks to be really effective, they had to be 'unrestricted', i.e. the U-boat commanders had to be allowed to attack without making any attempt to verify whether the target ship belonged to a belligerent power or not. In September 1915, after the Americans had made it quite clear that they wouldn't stand for this and would declare war if unrestricted attacks continued, the German admiralty had agreed to stop them. Part of their reason for doing so had been shortage of U-boats: with only twenty-five available at any one time, they couldn't wage an effective campaign anyway. Now there were enough – more than 100 – and the German admirals claimed that, free of restrictions, they could sink 600,000 tons of shipping a month. Six months of this would be enough to bring Britain to the edge of famine and the Allies' war machine to a halt. America would enter the war, true, but even if she did, it would be the middle of 1918 before she could intervene effectively and by then it would all be over.[1]

1. The only engagement between the British and German fleets took place in May 1916 off Jutland (the Danish Peninsula). The Germans did well in this and had some justification for claiming it as a tactical victory. But as they made it plain throughout the battle that getting home safely was their top priority, Jutland didn't alter the fact that it was the British fleet that commanded the sea.

Other events of 1916 include a major Russian advance in Caucasia and Germany's creation of a Polish kingdom out of territory conquered from the Russians (they didn't give this kingdom any of German Poland, nor did they give it a king). Portugal entered the war on the Allied side in the spring; the Greek government was forced to accept Allied direction in the summer.

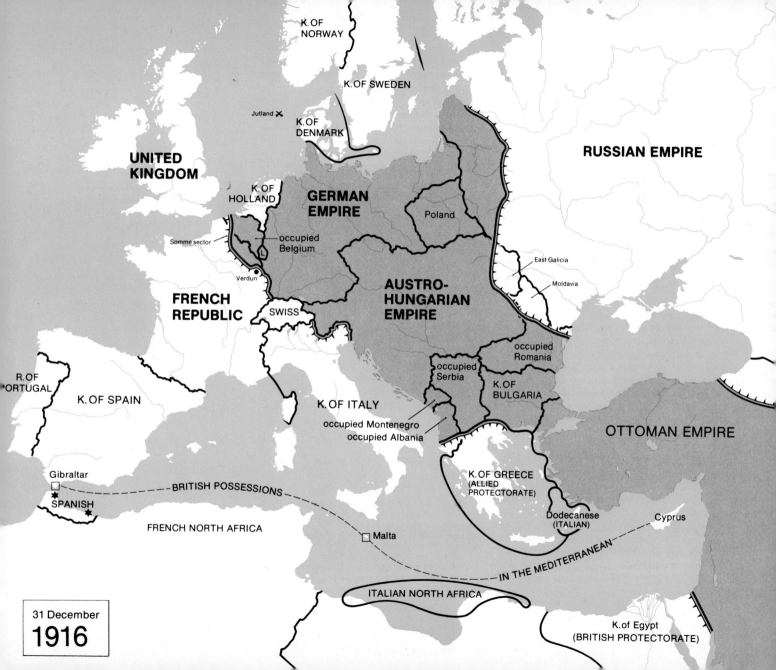

K. OF NORWAY

K. OF SWEDEN

Jutland ✕

K. OF DENMARK

UNITED KINGDOM

K. OF HOLLAND

GERMAN EMPIRE

RUSSIAN EMPIRE

Poland

Somme sector

occupied Belgium

East Galicia

Verdun

Moldavia

FRENCH REPUBLIC

AUSTRO-HUNGARIAN EMPIRE

SWISS

occupied Romania

occupied Serbia

K. OF ITALY

occupied Montenegro
occupied Albania

K. OF BULGARIA

R. OF PORTUGAL

K. OF SPAIN

OTTOMAN EMPIRE

Gibraltar

SPANISH

K. OF GREECE (ALLIED PROTECTORATE)

BRITISH POSSESSIONS

Dodecanese (ITALIAN)

Cyprus

FRENCH NORTH AFRICA

Malta

IN THE MEDITERRANEAN

ITALIAN NORTH AFRICA

K. of Egypt (BRITISH PROTECTORATE)

31 December
1916

THE U-BOAT CAMPAIGN began on 1 February 1917. At first everything went as planned, with the U-boats sinking the predicted 600,000 tons of shipping a month for six months. But the British then countered by introducing a convoy system which immediately cut the losses to a more tolerable 300,000 tons monthly. After this the U-boats never really got on top of the situation again: the tonnage sunk per U-boat per month gradually dropped back to the level ruling before restrictions were lifted, while the submariners' own losses mounted steadily. Far from winning the war, the U-boat enthusiasts had made certain that Germany would lose it, for, as a direct result of the campaign, America had joined the alliance against her in April.

If this wasn't appreciated at the time, it was because the German people sensed that – at long last – the land war was going their way. Russia was visibly wilting and it was clear that before long Germany would be able to dictate terms to her. France was almost as war-weary as Russia: her troops had actually mutinied after the failure of a much-touted offensive in April. There was every reason to believe that victory in the west would follow close on the heels of victory in the east.

Russia's decline had begun as soon as the peasantry had realized that the paper money the government was printing to pay for the war was in fact worthless. They refused to accept it, so the towns got no food. In March there were riots in Petrograd (St Petersburg);[1] when troops were called in to put down the rioters, they joined them instead. It was 1905 over again, with liberal politicians forming a parliamentary government and soviets springing up among the factory workers. This time, though, the Tsar was forced to abdicate.

Russia's new leaders were quick to assure the British and French that they would honour the alliance: the war would go on as though nothing had happened. But the capacity to wage war was no longer there: the support systems had disintegrated and the troops wouldn't fight anyway. The country drifted miserably along, its leaders helpless, their authority steadily waning.

One man did have a definite programme – Lenin, leader of the Bolsheviks. From the time he arrived in Petrograd in April (from Switzerland, where he had been in exile for many years), Lenin insisted that peace was his first priority, and he meant peace at any price. His supporters heard his views with dismay, his enemies with scorn, while the government branded him a traitor and he had to go into hiding. Over the next six months, however, the Petrograd Soviet came to see that this was what the country – and the revolution – needed. In November detachments of armed workers swept the Liberal government aside and put Lenin and his Bolsheviks in power. True to his word, he immediately asked the Germans for an armistice.[2]

Minor points to notice on this map are the additional progress made by the Germans in the east (in the Gulf of Livonia and Galicia), the lack of progress in the west (where the British had just sacrificed 300,000 men in a fruitless offensive in Flanders), the retreat of the Italians in the Veneto (following their rout in the Battle of Caporetto) and the British advance into Palestine (a very slow affair that had taken a year to get to the gates of Jerusalem).

1. During the wave of anti-German hysteria that swept the Allied countries in 1914 St Petersburg was renamed Petrograd. Another example of this sort of thing was provided by the British royal family, which changed its name from Saxe-Coburg-Gotha to Windsor.
2. Because the calendar in use in Russia at this time ran eleven days behind the western one, the two revolutions of 1917 are termed the February and October Revolutions.

K. OF
NORWAY

● Petrograd

K. OF SWEDEN

Gulf of Livonia

K. OF
DENMARK

RUSSIA

UNITED
KINGDOM

K. OF
HOLLAND

GERMAN EMPIRE

Poland

Flanders sector

occupied Belgium

Galicia

FRENCH
REPUBLIC

SWISS

Veneto

AUSTRO-
HUNGARIAN
EMPIRE

✕ Caporetto

occupied Romania

R. OF
ORTUGAL

K. OF SPAIN

occupied Montenegro

occupied
Serbia

K. OF
BULGARIA

K. OF ITALY

occupied Albania

OTTOMAN EMPIRE

Gibraltar

★ SPANISH ★

BRITISH POSSESSIONS

K. OF GREECE

FRENCH NORTH AFRICA

☐ Malta

Dodecanese
(ITALIAN)

Cyprus

IN THE MEDITERRANEAN

Jerusalem ●

ITALIAN NORTH AFRICA

K. of Egypt
(BRITISH PROTECTORATE)

30 November
1917

THE PEACE TERMS that Germany offered Lenin were very harsh: Russia would have to give up all claims to Poland, Lithuania, Finland and the Ukraine. Lenin had already recognized Finland's independence and he was prepared to see Poland and Lithuania go too – after all, they weren't ethnically Russian and he believed in separate states for separate peoples – but when it came to the Ukraine, even he had difficulty in keeping still: like all Russians, he regarded the Ukraine as part of the Motherland. Still, if this was the price of peace, then he would pay it.

The Germans sensed this and upped their demands. By August they were wanting the rest of the Baltic provinces (Estonia, Livonia and Kurland) and Georgia as well. They got them. By the time the ink was dry on this, the final version of the Treaty of Brest-Litovsk, Russia had lost a third of her productive land and a third of her people.

Lenin hoped that some at least of the territories he had ceded would maintain formal links with Soviet Russia. This idea wasn't in itself naive – the Finns, for example, would probably have ended up with a communist government if the Germans hadn't sent troops there to help the Whites (reactionaries) defeat the Reds (Bolsheviks). What was naive was to think that the Germans wouldn't interfere in this way. German forces quickly occupied all the ceded areas and made dependencies of them. Estonia, Livonia and Kurland were earmarked for eventual annexation; Finland, Lithuania, Poland, the Ukraine and Georgia were to be allowed local autonomy. No final decision was taken about the Crimea or Bessarabia, but the favoured plan was for the Crimea to become the nucleus of a detached Black Sea Province of the German Empire. Bessarabia would either be attached to this or go to the Romanians in compensation for their losses elsewhere.[1]

The Romanians badly needed some compensation. After the completion of the initial Brest-Litovsk negotiations (in March 1918) it was clearly their turn to sign on the dotted line; when they did so (in May), they lost the southern half of the Dobruja to the Bulgarians and the northern half to the Germans (another area to be included in the Black Sea Province?) besides having to make major frontier adjustments in favour of Austria-Hungary.

Hindenburg and Ludendorff had brought the war in the east to a successful conclusion; they now had to try to do the same in the west. And they had to do it by the summer of 1918, before the Americans appeared in France in strength. For the moment, after the transfer of the eastern armies to the west, the Germans had the superiority (200 German divisions to 170 British and French), but this would not last long. The critical blows must be struck in March and April.

By March Ludendorff had his troops in position: seventy specially trained 'assault divisions' faced thirty-five British on the Somme battle front. When the guns crashed out and the attack went in, the British line simply disintegrated: whole battalions vanished, never to be heard of again. Within a week the leading German formations had advanced forty miles, a penetration ten times better than anything the Allies had ever achieved. It was magnificent, but it wasn't enough. After a fortnight, the impetus had clearly gone out of the attack, German losses were beginning to exceed Allied and the offensive had to be closed down. The same thing happened with Ludendorff's second and third blows: they were tactical successes but strategic failures.

Ludendorff's third offensive took the Germans to the Marne again. Here, in early June, they were counter-attacked by American troops. There were only two divisions of them, but their impact was enormous. It was psychological as much as anything. By the reduced standards ruling at this stage of the war the American divisions were double strength. The men were fresh; their morale was high; most important of all, there were more where they came from. By the end of June there would be ten American divisions in the line: by the end of July, twenty; by the end of October, thirty.

Ludendorff's moment had come and gone.

1. The Germans actually occupied considerably more Russian territory than they were entitled to by the Brest-Litovsk treaty. They took Belorussia simply to shorten their line, but in the Black Sea region, where they advanced to the lower Don and crossed from the Crimea to the Taman Peninsula, they were clearly aiming at taking over permanently. In due course they would doubtless have imposed a third round of concessions on the Russian government.

Soviet power in this area was currently at a very low ebb. The Don Cossacks were refusing to recognize the authority of Moscow (the seat of the Soviet government since March, when Lenin had decided that the Germans were getting too close to Petrograd), the anti-Soviet forces rallying to the flag of General Denikin were proving more than a match for the local Bolsheviks and, in Caucasia, in the far south, the Turks had occupied not only the towns lost in 1878 – which they were entitled to by the Brest-Litovsk treaty – but everything else that wasn't already in German hands.

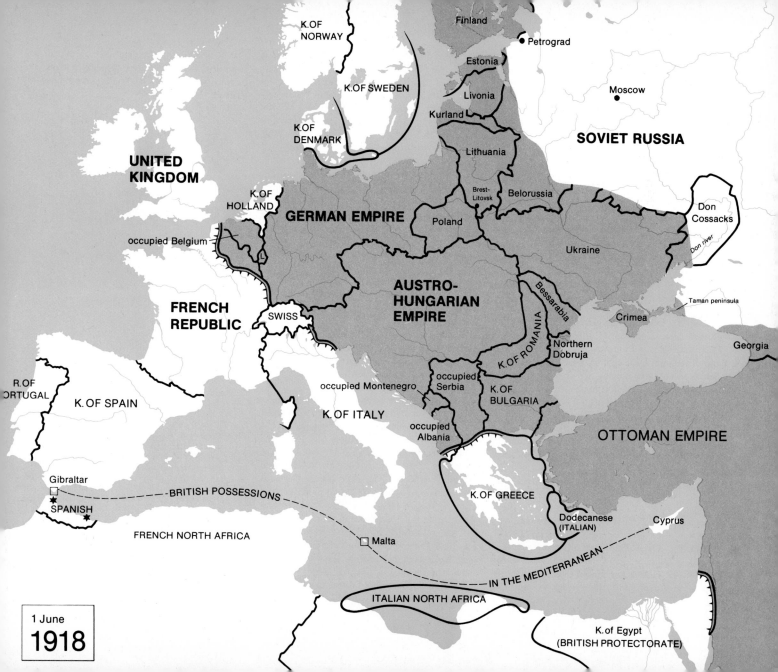

K.OF NORWAY

Finland

Petrograd

K.OF SWEDEN

Estonia

Moscow

Livonia

Kurland

SOVIET RUSSIA

UNITED KINGDOM

K.OF DENMARK

Lithuania

K.OF HOLLAND

GERMAN EMPIRE

Brest-Litovsk

Belorussia

Don Cossacks

occupied Belgium

Poland

Ukraine

Don river

FRENCH REPUBLIC

SWISS

AUSTRO-HUNGARIAN EMPIRE

Bessarabia

Taman peninsula

Crimea

R.OF PORTUGAL

K.OF SPAIN

K.OF ITALY

occupied Montenegro

occupied Serbia

K.OF ROMANIA

Northern Dobruja

Georgia

K.OF BULGARIA

OTTOMAN EMPIRE

occupied Albania

Gibraltar

SPANISH

BRITISH POSSESSIONS

K.OF GREECE

Dodecanese (ITALIAN)

Cyprus

FRENCH NORTH AFRICA

Malta

IN THE MEDITERRANEAN

ITALIAN NORTH AFRICA

K.of Egypt (BRITISH PROTECTORATE)

1 June
1918

IN JULY 1918 the last of Ludendorff's grand assaults petered out and the initiative on the western front passed to the Allies. Their local counter-attacks were so successful that they quickly developed them into a general offensive; if this never quite matched the pace Ludendorff had set in March, it was better sustained and so in the long run more effective. Every day the Germans had to withdraw somewhere along the line; every day the Allies completed the preparations for another local push. The tactical situation seems to have loosened up slightly: the attacks were expensive but not prohibitively so and, as the Allies ground steadily forward, week in, week out, the morale of the German army finally began to fray.

The signs of Germany's military decline were quickly read by her partners. In mid-September when the much ridiculed part-French, part-Serbian, part-British army in Greece mounted a major – and successful – attack on the German-led but mainly Bulgar forces opposite it, the Bulgars almost immediately decided to throw in their hand. By the end of the month the country was out of the war, British forces were moving across it towards the Turkish frontier, French columns had reached the Danube and the Serbs had made a good start on the liberation of their homeland. The Turks held out for a further month (during which the British conquered Syria), then they too surrendered. A Franco-British force sailed in triumph past Gallipoli and took possession of Constantinople.

The Allied armies in the Balkans still had a fair way to travel before they could bring Austria-Hungary under attack, but it was a journey they never had to make: the Habsburg Empire was falling to pieces of its own accord. October saw Czech nationalists take over in Prague and proclaim it the capital of an independent Czechoslovak state, while the Poles of Galicia announced their intention of taking the province into the new Polish state – a programme disputed by the Ruthenians of Eastern Galicia who looked towards the Ukrainian Republic. At the same time representatives of the various south-Slav peoples of the empire – Slovenes, Croats and Bosnians – repudiated Austro-Hungarian rule and expressed, with surprising unanimity, their desire to fuse with Serbia and Montenegro to form a single Yugoslav state. All that was left was for revolutions in Vienna and Budapest to declare in favour of separate Austrian and Hungarian republics and the Habsburg Empire had ceased to exist.

It was now early November. On the 3rd of the month the sailors of the German fleet mutinied rather than sail out on a death-or-glory mission against the British. The temper of many army divisions was reported to be equally uncertain. Reluctantly conceding that the war was lost, Kaiser Wilhelm abdicated on the 9th, leaving the way open for the signing of the armistice that America's President Wilson had indicated was on offer to the civilian leaders – not the military or the monarchy – of Germany. Any hopes that this armistice would take the form of a truce between equals were quickly dispelled by an examination of its terms: they amounted to complete surrender.[1]

There was only one mitigating circumstance. President Wilson had declared that the frontiers of post-war Europe would be decided by its people, not its politicians. Self-determination was to be the guiding principle; plebiscites would make clear the people's will. On this basis Germany wouldn't do too badly – which, of course, is why the Germans had chosen to negotiate with President Wilson and not his European allies. True, the President had indicated that there were exceptions to his general rule: Alsace-Lorraine would have to go back to France and the new Polish state – whose existence all parties had agreed on – must be given access to the sea; but if he stuck to his principles, Germany should emerge from the war clipped rather than shorn.

In Russia General Denikin was now in complete control of the Kuban area: his success marks the formal opening of the Civil War between Whites and Reds.

1. Of the three emperors who lost their crowns in the First World War, Kaiser Wilhelm did much the best: he lived in comfortable exile in Holland until his death aged eighty-two in 1941. Tsar Nicholas II, who had been placed under house arrest after the revolution of February 1917, was transferred to Ekaterinburg in the Urals by the Bolsheviks. When anti-Bolshevik forces advanced on the town in the summer of 1918, the local soviet had him (and his wife and children) shot.

The fate of Charles I of Austria was almost as ignominious. Forced to abdicate after a two-year reign (Franz Joseph had only died in 1916), he retired first to his Austrian estates, then, at Allied insistence, to Switzerland. In 1920 he made two unsuccessful attempts to seize power in Hungary, after which the Swiss refused to have him back. He died in penury in Madeira the following year.

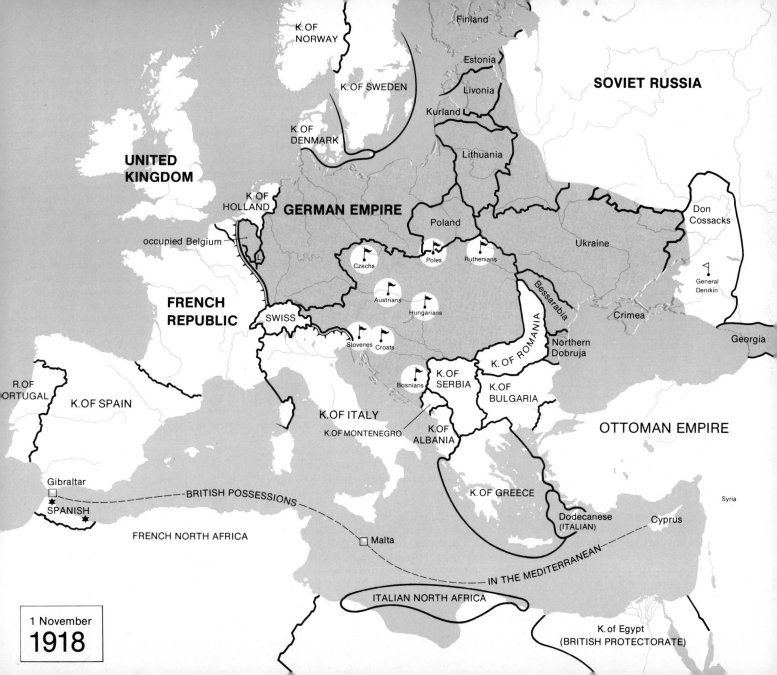

IN JANUARY 1919 the Allied leaders met at Versailles (under the chairmanship of President Wilson) and the peace conference began. In mapmaking terms the biggest task facing them was the carve-up of the defunct Austro-Hungarian Empire. This understandably led to considerable bickering among the successor states – Czechoslovakia, Austria, Hungary, Poland, Romania, Yugoslavia and Italy – and the Hungarians even tried fighting for a better deal. Their resistance, however, was quickly broken by the Romanians, who occupied Budapest in August (incidentally disposing of the only communist government to emerge in the postwar period, the dictatorship of Bela Kun). By October, apart from a few sectors where the final line was to be determined by a plebiscite, nearly all the new boundaries had been agreed.

An important exception was the frontier between Italy and Yugoslavia.[1] The Italians wanted Dalmatia (the eastern coast of the Adriatic), not because there were any Italians there – outside a few of the sea ports there were none at all – but because it had been an Italian possession during the Middle Ages and up to the end of the eighteenth century. And the British and French, when bidding for Italy's support in 1915, had said they could have it. Neither factor carried any weight with President Wilson: as far as he was concerned, the linguistic frontier was going to determine the political one and token concessions were all the Italians could expect.

Where President Wilson was prepared to compromise his self-determination principle was in cases where the physical geography seemed more important than the ethnic detail. For example, he let the Italians have the watershed line in the Alps, even though 250,000 Austrians lived south of it. And he agreed that the Czechoslovak frontier should run along the mountainous rim of Bohemia although the Germans inside this line – and there were two million of them – were known to be horrified at the idea.

These two exceptions had one unfortunate feature in common: they provided support for the view that the Wilson doctrine operated more favourably for the victors than for the vanquished. There were all these Germans in Czechoslovakia but no Czechs in Germany; there were the Austrians of the South Tyrol in Italy but no Italians in Austria; and, similarly, there were a lot of Magyars (ethnic Hungarians) in Romania but no Romanians in Hungary. However, the most glaring infringement of the self-determination principle was the prohibition of any union between Austria and Germany. One can see the Allies' point of view – they could hardly allow Germany to emerge from the war bigger than before – but it did make some of their finer phrases sound somewhat hypocritical.

The Germans, of course, made the most of this sort of inconsistency; when they signed the Treaty of Versailles they said quite openly that they were doing so under duress. But really they didn't do that badly, particularly if you consider how they had behaved to the Russians. They had to return Alsace-Lorraine to France, donate two large, but largely Polish, provinces (Posen and West Prussia) to the new Polish state and allow two of their Baltic ports (Danzig and Memel) to be re-graded as 'free cities'. But the other territories that the French and Poles asked for, Wilson put out to plebiscite – with the result that all of them bar the extreme tip of Upper Silesia eventually returned to the Reich.[2]

Bulgaria's losses were proportionately about the same as Germany's: she had to return the southern Dobruja to Romania, give Western Thrace to Greece and make some small frontier rectifications in Yugoslavia's favour. The Ottoman Empire got the same treatment as the Austro-Hungarian: it was completely dismantled. The exact details still hadn't been determined in October 1919, but the Arab areas were to be placed under British or French supervision (Palestine, Trans-Jordan and Iraq would go to the British, Syria and Cilicia to the French) and the Greeks were to get European Turkey up to the gates of Constantinople, though probably not Constantinople itself. The main question left to be decided was what would happen in Anatolia. Most of it would have to be left to the Turks, of course, but President Wilson wanted the Armenians to get a state of their own in the east and the Greeks wanted the Aegean coast (they had already put a force ashore at Smyrna). One thing was sure: whatever treaty the Allies decided on, the Sultan (in Constantinople) would sign it and the Turkish Nationalists (now setting up an opposition government in central Anatolia) would reject it. And in Mustapha Kemal, the hero of Gallipoli, the Turkish Nationalists had a leader to be reckoned with. Where he was in command, the Sultan's writ no longer ran – and neither did President Wilson's.

During the armistice negotiations the Allies had insisted on the Germans withdrawing from their conquests in the east; the unwelcome result of this was that the Bolsheviks occupied the Baltic states and the Ukraine. The Allied reaction was to beef up the White forces – General Yudenich's army in Estonia as well as General Denikin's in the south – and support them in counter-offensives that by October 1919 had taken Yudenich half-way to Petrograd and Denikin more than half-way to Moscow. At the same time the Poles occupied as much of western Russia as they could.

1. Until 1929 Yugoslavia was officially known as the Kingdom of the Serbs, Croats and Slovenes.
2. Allenstein and Marienwerder (the southern parts of East Prussia) voted in 1920, Upper Silesia in 1921–2 and the Saar (where the French insisted on a fifteen-year delay) in 1935. The Germans were also made to hold a plebiscite in northern Schleswig, something Bismarck had promised – but failed – to do in 1865; the voting took place in 1920 and resulted in most of it returning to Danish control.

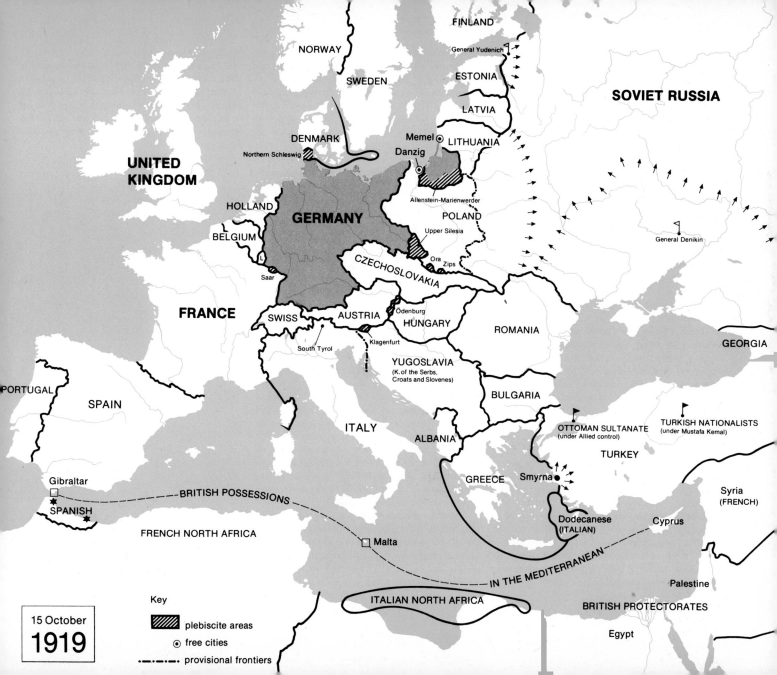

FINLAND

NORWAY

SWEDEN

SOVIET RUSSIA

General Yudenich

ESTONIA

LATVIA

UNITED KINGDOM

DENMARK

Memel ⊙ LITHUANIA

Northern Schleswig

Danzig ⊙

Allenstein-Marienwerder

HOLLAND

GERMANY

POLAND

General Denikin

BELGIUM

Upper Silesia

L

Saar

Ora Zips

CZECHOSLOVAKIA

FRANCE

SWISS

AUSTRIA

Ödenburg

HUNGARY

ROMANIA

GEORGIA

South Tyrol

Klagenfurt

YUGOSLAVIA
(K. of the Serbs,
Croats and Slovenes)

BULGARIA

PORTUGAL

SPAIN

ITALY

ALBANIA

OTTOMAN SULTANATE
(under Allied control)

TURKISH NATIONALISTS
(under Mustafa Kemal)

TURKEY

GREECE

Smyrna ●

Gibraltar □

BRITISH POSSESSIONS

Syria
(FRENCH)

★ SPANISH

★

Dodecanese
(ITALIAN)

Cyprus

FRENCH NORTH AFRICA

□ Malta

IN THE MEDITERRANEAN

Palestine

BRITISH PROTECTORATES

ITALIAN NORTH AFRICA

Egypt

15 October
1919

Key

▨ plebiscite areas

⊙ free cities

–·–·– provisional frontiers

THE WHITE OFFENSIVE in Russia collapsed with amazing speed: one month the White forces were closing in on Petrograd and Moscow, the next they were totally defeated and the re-organized Red Army was chasing them back to their starting points. But the Reds had to reckon with the Poles as well as the Whites: no sooner had the Bolsheviks entered the Ukrainian capital, Kiev, than a Polish army – in theory acting on behalf of the Ukrainian separatist movement – drove them out again (May 1920). However, the Poles didn't possess the resources for a campaign on this scale: a month later the Red Army recovered Kiev and it was Poland's turn to face invasion. The final round in this faintly absurd war – neither side was able to deploy more than the equivalent of ten divisions – was fought at the gates of Warsaw. Victory went to the Poles, which meant that they were able to resume control over the territories that they had taken the year before.

Lenin, who had been temporarily seduced by the vision of the Red Army spreading the revolution across Europe, now reverted to his Brest-Litovsk analysis. The overriding priority had to be the preservation of communism in Russia and if this meant recognizing the independence of Estonia, Latvia and Lithuania and giving the Poles most of what they wanted, he was prepared to do it. He was even prepared to acquiesce in Romania's occu-pation of Bessarabia. In 1920 and 1921 a whole batch of treaties regularized the existing state of affairs in eastern Europe. From a communist, as opposed to a Russian, point of view, the result wasn't entirely negative: the row of small and medium-sized countries along the Soviets' western border acted as a sort of *cordon sanitaire* between them and the hostile world of capitalism.

Every bit as embattled as the Bolsheviks at this time were the Turks; indeed in many ways their case was worse. The treaty finally presented to the Sultan by the Allies – and duly signed by him in 1920 – gave the Greeks all European Turkey bar Constanti-nople, plus, in Asia, the city of Smyrna and its hinterland. The treaty was, of course, repudiated by Mustapha Kemal's nationalist government, but the Greeks had been expecting that and had transferred the bulk of their army to Smyrna. From there, in 1921, they launched a full-scale offensive against the Kemalists; they got two-thirds of the way to Ankara, the nationalist headquarters, before they were stopped. But stopped they were, and, by the end of the year, the scales were tipping Kemal's way. He had secured his rear by eliminating the Armenian separatists and coming to terms with the Soviets and the French (in Syria); he had also scraped together enough men and material to begin planning a counter-offensive.[1]

Other changes since the last map include the elimination of an independent republic in the Caucasus (the Republic of Georgia) and the appear-ance of a new one in Ireland (the Irish Free State, or Eire). The Georgian Republic disappeared in 1921 as the Red Army mopped up the remnants of the White and separatist forces that had once held so much of the south. The Irish Republic was born out of a liberation struggle that had been going on for centuries, with the Catholic Irish usually failing to make much headway against the hated British oppressor. In the new climate of self-determination the British were prepared to give grudging recog-nition to Irish self-rule; however, the Protestants in the north of the island were not. The result was an unsatisfactory division between an independent republic (almost totally Catholic) in the south and a British province (largely Protestant) in the north.

This map also shows the treaty-makers' final ruling on the frontier between Yugoslavia and Italy. By this the Italians got Istria and the Yugoslavs Dalmatia except for Zara, which became an Italian enclave, and Fiume, which was declared a 'free city'. The 'free city' idea, which was really just a way of dodging the issue, didn't prove very successful. Of the three set up in 1919–20, Memel was annexed by the Lithuanians at the beginning of 1923 and Fiume by the Italians later the same year. The third – Danzig – survived until the Second World War, but its status was constantly in dispute and its existence harmed rather than helped Polish-German relations.

1. Despite Turkey's weakness the settlements with both Russia and France were in her favour. Lenin, extending his peace-at-any-price formula, let Kemal keep the Caucasian towns recovered by the Turks at Brest-Litovsk. The French, who were having trouble with Arab nationalists in Syria, were prepared to purchase Kemal's neutrality by turning Cilicia over to him.

NORWAY

FINLAND

Petrograd

SWEDEN

ESTONIA

LATVIA

EIRE

DENMARK

Memel
Danzig

LITHUANIA

SOVIET RUSSIA

UNITED
KINGDOM

HOLLAND

GERMANY

Warsaw

POLAND

Kiev

BELGIUM

CZECHOSLOVAKIA

Saar

Bessarabia

FRANCE

SWISS

AUSTRIA

HUNGARY

ROMANIA

Istria
Fiume

YUGOSLAVIA
(K. of the Serbs,
Croats and Slovenes)

Zara

BULGARIA

OTTOMAN
SULTANATE
(under Allied control)

PORTUGAL

SPAIN

ITALY

ALBANIA

TURKISH
NATIONALISTS
(under Mustafa Kemal)

Cilicia

Smyrna

Gibraltar

SPANISH

GREECE

Syria
(FRENCH)

BRITISH POSSESSIONS

Dodecanese
(ITALIAN)

Cyprus

FRENCH NORTH AFRICA

Malta

IN THE MEDITERRANEAN

Palestine

ITALIAN NORTH AFRICA

BRITISH PROTECTORATES

Egypt

31 December
1921

KEMAL'S COUNTER-OFFENSIVE broke the Greek army in Anatolia surprisingly quickly and completely. Perhaps half of it managed to get back to Smyrna, but the Turks closed up fast and the Greek dream of reviving the Byzantine Empire ended in a hurried and humiliating evacuation. Kemal then turned his attention to the Straits, where the Allies had said they were going to set up an international zone. Confronted with a Turkish army that was clearly spoiling for a fight, they soon changed their minds; as the Greeks had decided they wouldn't even try to hold on to East Thrace, the part of the 1920 treaty that dealt with this area became a dead letter: the Turks simply reoccupied everything they had held in 1914.[1]

The new Turkey had no pretensions to Empire: it accepted that its position was that of a middle-rank power. There were more of these now: Poland, Romania, Czechoslovakia and Yugoslavia all came in the same category. Whether this was a good thing for the stability of Europe is debatable: these countries were the main beneficiaries of the Versailles settlement, but none of them was strong enough to contribute much to its defence so the responsibility for maintaining the peace fell, as ever, on the major powers.

The balance between these was in a peculiar state. Whatever President Wilson had thought his country's post-war role should be, the US Senate had decided that there would be no American commitment to Europe. And Russia had become a quite uncertain quantity. So the task of keeping Germany in line – a Germany that had been irritated but not weakened by its territorial losses – fell entirely on France and Britain. The question was, were they up to it?

The French thought not. The only way they could see themselves coping was by using the advantage of the moment to cripple Germany permanently. At their insistence, special clauses were inserted into the Versailles treaty limiting the German army to 100,000 men (seven divisions) and forbidding it the use of heavy weapons; other sections of the treaty restricted the German navy to a few small surface ships and abolished the air force altogether. Finally, the German economy was loaded with such a burden of reparations that it would be twenty years before any German could afford to think of guns or glory again.[2]

The British were vaguely aware that punishing the new, relatively liberal and pacific German Republic for the sins of the Wilhelmine Empire was a policy that could backfire: the more grievances the German people had, the more likely they were to turn to the parties of the extreme right. And there were plenty of these about, many of them including uniformed cadres of bully boys. One was Adolf Hitler's Nazi party, which had a brief moment of glory in 1923 when Ludendorff was persuaded into joining it in an attempt to seize power in Bavaria. However, the coup was such a miserable flop that the Nazi party faded badly over the next few years. Even in 1928, when it made something of a comeback, it wasn't able to claim a membership of more than 100,000 or win more than a bare dozen of the 491 seats in the Reichstag.[3]

This was a far less successful record than that of the equivalent party in Italy, the black-shirted *Fascisti*. Largely through the weakness of the Italian king, the Fascist leader Benito Mussolini was able to seize the reins of government in 1922. Within a few years he had turned Italy into a one-party state and was beginning to make threatening gestures towards some of the smaller countries abroad. It should have been more alarming than it was, but Italians dressing up and shouting slogans was something the world could live with. And whatever people might say about Mussolini *personally*, at least he made the trains run on time.

1. Kemal spent the rest of his life trying to secularize and modernize Turkey. A minor aspect of this was a decree enjoining all Turks to take surnames (as opposed to patronymics) and it was to set an example of this that he took the name by which he is now remembered, Ataturk (Father of the Turks).

2. After the war of 1870–71 the French had paid the Germans an indemnity equivalent (at 1919 prices) to £500 million; now Germany was presented with a bill for £6,850 million. According to the best financial opinion of the time (meaning Keynes), the most Germany could possibly pay was £2,000 million.

3. Nazi is a contraction of National Socialist (*National Sozialist*). The brown-shirted paramilitary force that formed the backbone of the movement was known as the S.A. (from *Sturm Abteilungen*, meaning Storm Troopers); the especially tough and trustworthy were given black uniforms and acted as Hitler's bodyguard (*Schutzstaffel*, hence S.S.).

FINLAND 3.75M

NORWAY
2.75M

SWEDEN 6M

Scotland
4.75m

Northern Ireland
1.25m

ESTONIA 1M

LATVIA 2M

Great Russia 75m

EIRE 3M

UNITED
KINGDOM
46M

DENMARK
3.5M

Danzig
0.4m

LITHUANIA
2.5M

USSR 155M

England and Wales
40m

HOLLAND
8M

Belorussia
5m

Siberia and
Turkestan
35m

GERMANY
66M

POLAND 32M

BELGIUM
8M

Ukraine and Crimea 30m

LUXEMBOURG
0.3M

CZECHOSLOVAKIA
14.75M

FRANCE
42M

SWISS
4M

AUSTRIA
6.5M

HUNGARY
8.75M

ROMANIA 18M

Caucasia 10m

PORTUGAL
6.5M

SPAIN 23M

YUGOSLAVIA 14M

BULGARIA
6M

ITALY 41M

ALBANIA
1M

TURKEY 16M

GREECE 6.25M

DODECANESE
0.1M

CYPRUS
0.25M

SYRIA 3M

MOROCCO 6.5M
Spanish sector 1m)

ALGERIA 6.5M

MALTA 0.25M

TUNISIA
2.5M

PALESTINE
AND
TRANS-
JORDAN
1.25M

EGYPT 15M

LIBYA 0.75M

Population
1930

EVERY COUNTRY had its economic difficulties in the immediate post-war years, but in two – Germany and Russia – the difficulties were crippling. In Russia the cumulative effects of war, revolution and the harvest failures of 1920 and 1921 had emptied the cities and ruined the countryside; things were so bad that, given anything in the way of a breathing space, they had to get better. Lenin, seeing this, decided to let nature take its course. He called off the emergency system of expropriations ('War Communism'), by which the government had kept itself going, and instituted a New Economic Policy (NEP) that made small-scale private enterprise legal again. It was enough to do the trick. The NEPmen, as the hard-line Communists slightly referred to them, slowly brought life back to factory and farm and by 1924, the year of Lenin's death, production was back to something like two-thirds of the pre-war level.

Germany's problem was financial. The Kaiser's government had never made any effort to pay for the war because reparations from the Allies were expected to cover the deficit. Now the boot was on the other foot: the Allies were presenting their bills for the Germans to pay – and that at a time when the exchequer was hopelessly overdrawn. There was nothing for it but to print enough paper money to inflate away the internal debt and borrow enough abroad to pay the foreign creditors. This sounds straightforward enough, but the social cost was very high: inflation pauperized the middle class, while a delay in just one of the reparations payments brought a French occupation of the Ruhr that paralysed much of German industry in 1923–4. In the late 1920s Germany finally regained its pre-war level of output, but, of course, the opposition hadn't stood still in the interim. In motor cars, for example, Germany had once led the world: now her industry was turning out less vehicles (about 90,000 a year)

than either the British or French (about 200,000 a year each).

The difference between these figures is significant; even more so is the difference between them and America's. Whereas the Europeans measured their production by the hundred thousand, the Americans measured theirs by the million – to be exact, four millions in 1928 and five millions in 1929. Indeed the scale of the American economy was now so vast that Europe's was effectively subordinate to it. But in 1929 the American system suddenly went wildly wrong. A downturn in the business cycle caught the market there so over-extended that there was a progressive collapse – on the stockmarket, in the banking world and in the world of commerce. As the flow of goods came to a halt and the factories closed, the dole queues lengthened. By the early 1930s there were twenty-five million unemployed in the United States and, largely as a secondary effect of this disaster, three million unemployed in Britain and six million in Germany.

This was one blow more than Germany's social structure could stand. In the 1932 elections the Nazis increased their number of seats in the Reichstag to 230, becoming the largest single party. Hindenburg, now President of the Republic, had sworn that he would never ask Hitler to form a government, but the new generation of army leaders talked him round. In 1933 Hitler became Chancellor, an office he soon transformed into the autocratic position of Führer (Leader). He solved the unemployment problem by starting an immense rearmament programme. At the same time he dispelled the army's fear that he might put the S.A. above the traditional services by using the S.S. to massacre the more independent-minded of the S.A. leaders. He also dropped clear hints as to what all this rearmament was for: he intended to obtain for his empire – the 'Third Reich' – resources on a continental scale.

In practical terms this could mean only one thing,

expansion eastward into Russia. No one read Hitler's mind with greater clarity than Joseph Stalin, the Bolshevik leader who had now established himself as Lenin's successor. Presenting his plans for the forced industrialization of Russia, he told his followers: 'We are fifty or a hundred years behind the advanced countries and we must make good this gap in ten years. Either we do it, or they crush us.'

It seemed an impossible task. In the late 1920s Russia was producing, as it had in 1914, about half as much steel as the United Kingdom, which in turn was producing about half as much as Germany. Yet by 1937, when the second of Stalin's five-year plans was completed, the gap had been virtually closed: Russia was turning out considerably more steel than Britain and very nearly as much as Germany. The achievement is visible on the map: Stalin's new industrial centres are dotted across what had been, only a short time before, the empty quarter of the continent.

The cost in human terms is almost unbelievable. The peasantry, who had to provide the initial resources, were plundered and left to starve. Much of the labour needed was obtained by arbitrary arrest and most of those arrested were callously worked to death. More than a million people were shot out of hand; ten times as many died in the camps. To save his people from the Nazis, Stalin murdered, beat and brutalized them in a reign of terror that even Hitler would have difficulty matching.

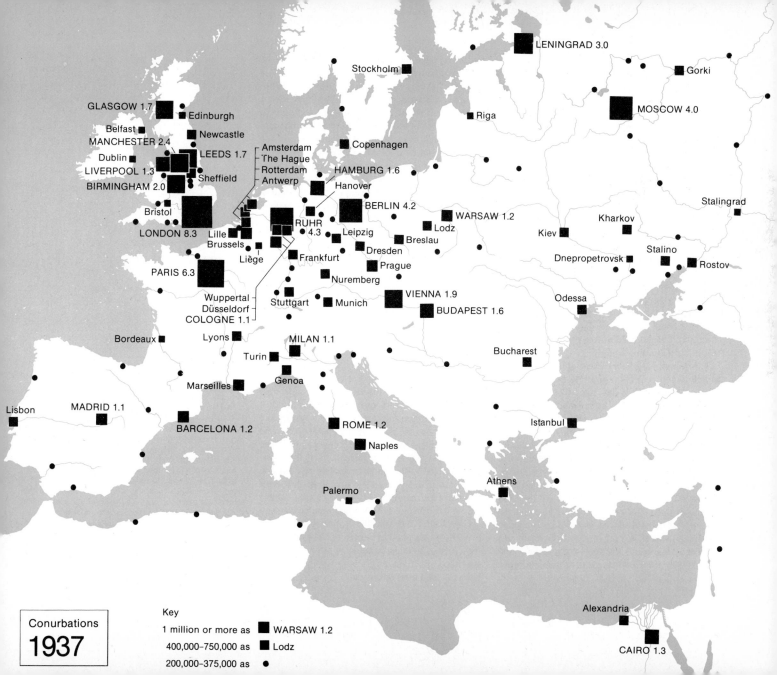

GLASGOW 1.7
Edinburgh
Belfast
Newcastle
MANCHESTER 2.4
LEEDS 1.7
Dublin
LIVERPOOL 1.3
Sheffield
BIRMINGHAM 2.0
Bristol
LONDON 8.3
Lille
Brussels
Liège
PARIS 6.3

Amsterdam
The Hague
Rotterdam
Antwerp
HAMBURG 1.6
Hanover
BERLIN 4.2
RUHR 4.3
Leipzig
Breslau
Dresden
Frankfurt
Prague
Nuremberg
Wuppertal
Düsseldorf
COLOGNE 1.1
Stuttgart
Munich
VIENNA 1.9
BUDAPEST 1.6

Stockholm
Copenhagen
Riga
WARSAW 1.2
Lodz

LENINGRAD 3.0
Gorki
MOSCOW 4.0
Stalingrad
Kharkov
Kiev
Stalino
Dnepropetrovsk
Rostov
Odessa
Bucharest

Bordeaux
Lyons
MILAN 1.1
Turin
Genoa
Marseilles

Istanbul

Lisbon
MADRID 1.1
BARCELONA 1.2
ROME 1.2
Naples

Athens

Palermo

Alexandria
CAIRO 1.3

Conurbations
1937

Key

1 million or more as   ■ WARSAW 1.2

400,000–750,000 as   ■ Lodz

200,000–375,000 as   ●

DURING THE LATE 1930s it was obvious to everyone that the war clouds were gathering: Hitler was turning Germany into an armed camp and in his smaller way Mussolini was looking for trouble too. In the Far East, Japan was making menacing moves. But whatever Hitler might intend ultimately, he couldn't build Germany's armed forces up to battle strength before 1938 and it was an unexpected flare-up in Spain in 1936 that first brought the forces of Fascism and democracy (or was it communism?) into open conflict. Franco, the Spanish general who led the right-wing revolt against the not very competent left-wing government of Spain, quickly got the upper hand in this fighting. During 1937 he completed the conquest of the north; in 1938 he split the remaining republican territory into two halves by driving through to the Mediterranean. The next year's campaign was to bring him complete victory. By then half a million Spaniards had died, more of them in the mass executions that both sides were prone to indulge in than in the front-line fighting.[1]

This brings us to Hitler's year of decision, which turned out to be 1939, not 1938. That wasn't for want of bellicosity on his part, for he was now pushing as hard and fast as he could. In February 1938 he declared that he was not prepared to tolerate the separation of Austria from Germany any longer and in March, by a combination of threats and cajolery, he persuaded the Austrian government to let German troops into the country in advance of the plebiscite that was to decide the issue. The results of this would have been more convincing if they had been a bit under the 99 per cent Yes vote that the Nazi press later announced, but there was enough substance to the claim that union with Germany was what most Austrians wanted to give Britain and France the excuse they needed for doing nothing. After all, they had already done nothing about

Hitler's repudiation of the arms-limitation clauses of the Versailles treaty.

Czechoslovakia was a different case. When Hitler declared (in September) that another thing he wasn't prepared to tolerate any longer was Czechoslovak 'mistreatment' of the German minority in Bohemia, it was difficult to see how a general European war could be avoided. If the German army crossed the Czech border, the Czechs would certainly fight, because the French and Russians had promised them their full support. And the British would almost inevitably join the anti-German coalition too.

At least that was what everyone thought. But at the last moment the British Prime Minister, Neville Chamberlain, made a personal intervention. He possessed in full the loathing and fear of war which characterized the British in the inter-war period. He recognized that Germany had genuine grievances and persuaded himself that if these were met a repeat of the 1914–18 holocaust could be avoided. On his own initiative he flew to Munich and talked a reluctant Hitler into calling off his attack in return for the parts of Czechoslovakia where the German minority lived. The French were relieved to let Chamberlain play out his idea; the Russians said nothing and the Czechs, knowing that they couldn't fight alone, bit their lips and signed the agreement.

It was a terrible decision. If Chamberlain was right and Hitler's ambitions were now satisfied, well and good. But if Hitler wanted more than a pan-German state – if he wanted hegemony over Europe – then an immense military advantage had been surrendered. Czechoslovakia's defence line – mountains and fortifications both – had been given away and as a result Czechoslovakia's army of twenty-five divisions was as good as written off. Moreover, the Franco-Russian understanding, which had been the best hope of containing the expansion of Nazi Germany, had been destroyed.[2]

1. The Spanish Republic had come into existence in 1931, when a popular rebellion forced King Alfonso XIII to flee. The Republicans then attempted to push Spain from the eighteenth century into the twentieth in one go, a programme that alienated the church, the army and the upper classes and finally precipitated Franco's rebellion.

Franco received important, but probably not critical, help from Hitler and Mussolini; the Republicans got a bit of help – not enough to make any difference – from Stalin, and rather more from the international communist movement which sponsored the volunteer International Brigades.

2. To make it appear that the Munich agreement wasn't just a matter of knuckling under to Hitler, the Czechs were forced to give up other areas which contained significant minorities. The Poles got the town of Teschen and the Hungarians a strip along the southern border of Slovakia, where the population was largely Magyar.

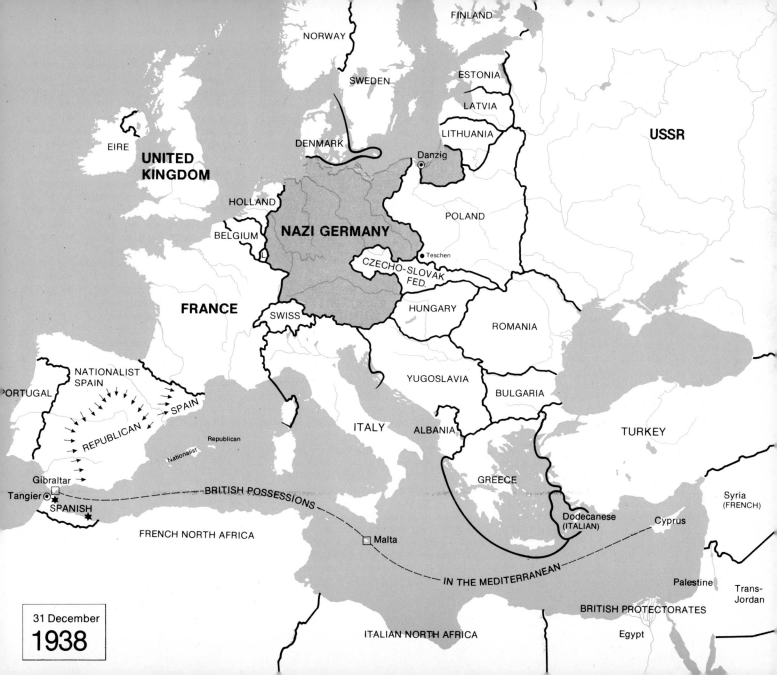

FINLAND

NORWAY

SWEDEN

ESTONIA

LATVIA

EIRE

UNITED KINGDOM

DENMARK

Danzig

LITHUANIA

USSR

HOLLAND

NAZI GERMANY

POLAND

BELGIUM

Teschen

FRANCE

CZECHO-SLOVAK FED.

SWISS

HUNGARY

ROMANIA

NATIONALIST SPAIN

PORTUGAL

SPAIN

REPUBLICAN

Republican

Nationalist

YUGOSLAVIA

BULGARIA

ITALY

ALBANIA

TURKEY

Gibraltar

Tangier

SPANISH

BRITISH POSSESSIONS

GREECE

Dodecanese (ITALIAN)

Cyprus

FRENCH NORTH AFRICA

Malta

Syria (FRENCH)

IN THE MEDITERRANEAN

Palestine

Trans-Jordan

BRITISH PROTECTORATES

ITALIAN NORTH AFRICA

Egypt

31 December
1938

WHILE NEVILLE CHAMBERLAIN was telling the British how he had returned from Munich bearing 'peace with honour', Adolf Hitler was putting the finishing touches to his plans for removing Czechoslovakia from the map. First he encouraged the Slovaks and Ruthenians to declare their independence of the Czecho-Slovak Federation; then he browbeat the Czech government into asking for German intervention 'to prevent a civil war'; finally he moved in (March 1939). The scheme was clever – Germany's enemies had no legal grounds for their protests – but it was also transparent. No one now had any doubt about Hitler's intentions.

Nor was there much doubt as to who his next victim was going to be. Poland had gained more German territory at Versailles than any other country; the existence of Danzig and of the Polish corridor that separated East Prussia from the rest of Germany were standing affronts to German nationalism. When Hitler opened his propaganda campaign against these 'injustices', Chamberlain, in a joint declaration with the French, finally drew the line: if Germany invaded Poland, Britain and France would declare war. However, because both he and the Poles shrank from asking the Russians to join this anti-Nazi alliance – the Poles because they knew exactly the price the Russians would ask (the return of the territory Poland had annexed in 1919–20), Chamberlain because he couldn't bring himself to associate with Bolsheviks – the Anglo-French threat was not all that impressive. As Winston Churchill, Chamberlain's main antagonist in the British parliament, pointed out, it would take a two-front war to make the German military think twice and without Russia there wouldn't be an eastern front for long.

Actually, Hitler wouldn't have been deterred by any combination: he had already set the date for the invasion of Poland. However, the Nazi leader did sense that this was the moment to make an offer to Stalin. Why not let him have the eastern half of Poland if he promised to keep out of the coming war? Stalin, angry and alarmed at the Allies' attitude to him and his regime, accepted – with conditions. As well as eastern Poland he asked for, and got, a free hand in Estonia, Latvia and Bessarabia. A week after the finishing touches had been put to this agreement, the German army crossed the Polish frontier (1 September).

Hitler may have been eager for war, but even he didn't want another bloody slogging match like the First World War. Nor did his generals. But how could the immense fire power that automatic weapons had brought to the battlefield be countered? There was a general agreement that the only possible answer was the tank, a British invention that had been used with some success by the Allies in the closing phase of the First World War. There was also general agreement that tanks should be employed as they had been then, in support of the infantry. However, Germany's General Guderian had a quite different idea. During the 1920s he worked out a plan for motorizing and armouring the elements of a normal division – infantry, artillery, signals and engineers – so that they could work alongside tanks without slowing them down; they and the tanks would then be combined to form a special panzer (meaning 'armoured') division. Panzer divisions would be very expensive – to make them possible, the rest of the German army would have to go on making do with horse-drawn transport – but Guderian believed that with half a dozen of them he could make war a matter of movement again.

The year Hitler came to power, Guderian showed him the first experimental panzer unit. 'That's what I want,' cried an excited Führer, who there and then gave the panzer concept his full backing. As a result, all six of the armoured divisions called for in Guderian's initial programme were ready in time for the invasion of Poland. They were grouped into three panzer corps: one, under Guderian's personal command, in the north; two, under Generals Hoepner and Kleist, in the south. All were under orders to drive on Warsaw as fast as possible.

The insistence on forward speed made the campaign against Poland a model operation: Hoepner's tanks were at the gates of the Polish capital within a week; Poland's armies, strung along the frontier in First World War style, found themselves isolated, outflanked and then surrounded as German infantry poured through the breaches the panzers had made. The world had its first taste of *Blitzkrieg* – 'lightning war'. It also had its first experience of Nazi terror as the Germans ruthlessly bombed and shelled Warsaw into submission.

The newspapers made banner headlines of the siege of Warsaw. What they missed was the fact that Guderian wasn't there. He had never thought Warsaw a suitable objective for his panzers and had managed to get Brest-Litovsk, 120 miles further east, put in his orders instead. He reached the town on 14 September and three days later, forty miles to the south of it, established contact with the leading elements of Kleist's corps. This was the sort of manoeuvre he was interested in, an envelopment on a really massive scale.[1]

1. Hitler had forced the Lithuanians to return Memel to Germany in March; Mussolini, with the Führer's approval, had occupied Albania in April; in June the Turks had used the deepening crisis in Europe to extract Antioch from the French authorities in Syria.

FINLAND

NORWAY

SWEDEN

ESTONIA

LATVIA

LITHUANIA

USSR

DENMARK

Danzig

Guderian

Brest-Litovsk

Warsaw

EIRE

UNITED
KINGDOM

HOLLAND

NAZI
GERMANY

POLAND

BELGIUM

L

Hoepner
Kleist

Bohemia-Moravia

Slovakia

FRANCE

SWISS

HUNGARY

ROMANIA

PORTUGAL

SPAIN

YUGOSLAVIA

BULGARIA

TURKEY

ITALY

Albania

Gibraltar

Tangier

SPANISH

BRITISH POSSESSIONS

GREECE

Antioch

Syria
(FRENCH)

Dodecanese
(ITALIAN)

Cyprus

FRENCH NORTH AFRICA

Malta

IN THE MEDITERRANEAN

Palestine

Trans-
Jordan

BRITISH PROTECTORATES

ITALIAN NORTH AFRICA

Egypt

17 September
1939

BECAUSE OF Guderian's advance to Brest-Litovsk the Germans ended up with rather more of Poland than their agreement with Stalin entitled them to. However, the Soviet dictator didn't make any difficulties about this; he just said that, in compensation, he'd like Lithuania added to his 'sphere of interest'. Hitler agreed and by the end of the year there were Red Army units in all three of the Baltic republics. There were also Russian troops in Finland, though only just. Ordered in by Stalin in November after Finland had refused to alter its frontier for him, most of them had been disposed of by spirited Finnish counter-attacks. Not till February 1940 did the Red Army prove able to bludgeon its way forward to the line Stalin wanted.[1]

Stalin's pact with Hitler and the ruthless way he exploited it aroused great fury in the west: indeed, during the Russo-Finnish War, anti-Russian feeling ran so high that Britain and France – as though they hadn't enough on their plates – actually planned to send an expeditionary force to the aid of the Finns. This force could only have been deployed with the consent of the Norwegians and Swedes (which was refused), but the fact that the expedition had been mooted at all started people thinking. Three-quarters of Germany's iron ore came from northern Scandinavia; if the Allies could get control of this region – and they now had an expeditionary force available to do the job – Germany would be starved of a vital resource. Both sides saw this at much the same time, but as usual it was Hitler who moved first. Combined air and sea landings in April gave him control of Denmark and most of Norway and, though the British started out confident that their command of the sea would give them the edge in the campaign, it was command of the air that decided it. The Germans had the airfields; they soon had the rest of Norway.

Meanwhile, all was quiet on the western front. To most people this inactivity was inexplicable.

Western journalists, who had been expecting something like 1914, began writing about the 'phoney war' and even Germans remarked on the contrast between the *Blitzkrieg* in Poland and the *'Sitzkrieg'* in the west. But whereas the French were deliberately holding back – they felt that the right policy, at least initially, was defensive – the German generals had orders from the Führer to attack at the earliest possible moment. Their trouble was that they simply couldn't get the troops ready for the offensive – a replay of the Schlieffen Plan – before May 1940.

By the time they were ready, the plan had been changed. A German plane carrying a complete copy of the original orders had crash-landed in Belgium, forcing the High Command to come up with something new. Of the various ideas discussed, the one judged best used the Schlieffen manoeuvre as a way of getting the Allies to extend their line but put the main blow in the centre, through Luxembourg. The aim was to split the Allied front in two.

The German army had ten panzer divisions available by now; Guderian, with three of them, had the task of making the crucial breakthrough. The whole operation went like clockwork. The Allied generals matched the German move forward in the Low Countries (Holland as well as Belgium this time) but didn't pay much attention to anything else. On the fifth day of the offensive, when the Allies were fully committed to the Belgian front, Guderian struck. His two lead divisions broke out of the bridgeheads they had established on the Meuse and raced for the Channel. Six days later – ten days after the beginning of the offensive – they were there. The Allied front was irretrievably broken.

Hitler and his generals now had a choice: they could concentrate on eliminating the Allied armies to the north or they could turn south and conquer France. They chose the second course. This allowed the British to lift off most of their men via the one French port remaining to them, Dunkirk, but it meant a speedy doom for France. Hoth took his

panzer corps across the north of the country; Kleist and Guderian, each now in command of a four-division panzer group, drove south. The French in the frontier fortifications – the famed 'Maginot Line' – found their guns were pointing the wrong way. On the 22 June the French government, recognizing that the military position was hopeless, made its formal submission.[2]

Success on this scale was enough to turn anyone's head, but Hitler seemed calmer than usual. He still had Britain to settle with, after all. And then there was Russia. If he had forgotten about Stalin in these exciting days, he now got a nasty reminder. At the end of June the Soviet dictator told the Romanians that he wanted Bessarabia and northern Bukovina. Bessarabia had been promised him in the Nazi-Soviet pact, but no one had said anything about Bukovina. Hitler, fully committed as he was in the west, couldn't do anything except advise the Romanians to submit, but he wasn't at all pleased.

1. The Finns were then forced to cede this territory, but they were allowed to keep their freedom. In this they were more fortunate than the inhabitants of the Baltic republics, who were soon completely absorbed into the Soviet system.

2. Mussolini, finally persuaded that Germany was going to win the war, came in on her side on 10 June.

FINLAND

occupied
Norway

SWEDEN

occupied
Denmark

USSR

EIRE

UNITED
KINGDOM

HOLLAND

Dunkirk • BELGIUM

NAZI GERMANY

Poland

H

K

G

Guderian

Bohemia-
Moravia

Slovakia

Northern
Bukovina

Bessarabia

FRANCE

SWISS

HUNGARY

ROMANIA

PORTUGAL

SPAIN

YUGOSLAVIA

BULGARIA

TURKEY

ITALY

Albania

Gibraltar

Tangier ⊙
★
SPANISH
★

— BRITISH POSSESSIONS

GREECE

Dodecanese
(ITALIAN)

Cyprus

Syria
(FRENCH)

FRENCH NORTH AFRICA

□ Malta

— IN THE MEDITERRANEAN

Palestine

Trans-
Jordan

ITALIAN NORTH AFRICA

BRITISH PROTECTORATES

Egypt

Key

Invasion of France, second phase

H   Hoth

K   Kleist

G   Guderian

30 June
1940

WITH FRANCE DEFEATED, Hitler had no wish to prolong the war in the west: his interest lay in Russia. However, it takes two to make peace and Churchill, who had replaced Chamberlain as Britain's Prime Minister in April 1940, spurned the Führer's overtures. Willy-nilly, Hitler had to plan for an invasion of the British Isles. This wasn't a simple proposition: the British not only had a navy to protect their shores; they also had – and it was the one military preparation they had got exactly right – radar-directed fighter squadrons to protect their skies. In the Battle of Britain Hitler signally failed to win the air superiority he needed; in September, 'Operation Sealion', the invasion of Britain, had to be indefinitely postponed. The Nazi leader shrugged off the defeat as irrelevant; within three months his signature was on the preliminary directive for 'Operation Barbarossa', the invasion of Russia.

In the meantime Mussolini made his play for the limelight, invading Greece (from Albania) and Egypt (from Libya). Both offensives quickly turned into humiliating routs: by early 1941 the Greeks had occupied the southern third of Albania and the British most of Libya. Hitler, who had been particularly keen to have the Balkans quiet at this juncture, was furious, but felt he had to bail out his fellow dictator. And, because the Yugoslavs refused to allow German troops transit to the Greek theatre, he decided he must occupy Yugoslavia too.

Five panzer divisions and ten days sufficed for the conquest of Yugoslavia, a week more for mainland Greece. Then a whirlwind airborne assault on Crete completed Germany's mastery of the Aegean and the total discomfiture of the forces Britain had dispatched to the area. At the same time the two panzer divisions of Rommel's Afrika Corps restored the Italian position in Libya.

These diversions, plus the sheer scale of the preparations, caused a five-week postponement of the invasion of Russia. Stalin refused to heed the many warning signs and when the onslaught began (on 22 June 1941), his surprise was total. The four panzer groups commanded by Hoepner, Hoth, Guderian and Kleist swept through the frontier zone and into the vastness of Russia.

The northern German thrust was the least successful. The country wasn't really suitable for tanks and, though Hoepner's panzers were never held up for long, the Russians managed to keep their formations intact as they fell back on Leningrad; at this point, Hoepner's group was withdrawn and it was left to the German and Finnish infantry to close the ring round the city.

On the central front Hoth and Guderian had greater resources than Hoepner, more suitable terrain and a fabulous initial opportunity, which they seized with both hands. Their two panzer groups raced along parallel roads north and south of the main Russian concentration, finally swinging in behind it just east of Minsk. By the fifth day of the invasion they had thirty Russian divisions in the bag, a force that was pounded to bits by German support troops over the next three weeks. By then Guderian and Hoth were through the next Russian line and closing in again, this time on the Russian reserve armies. This second pincer snapped shut on 16 July when the lead tanks of Guderian's group entered Smolensk; once again the Russian divisions so contained – about a dozen of them – were left for the German infantry to finish off.

The southern arm of the German invasion suffered some of the same disadvantages as the northern, in that it had only a single panzer group and no obvious 'pincer movement' to make. Yet in early August Kleist succeeded in getting behind the bulk of the Russian first-line armies and pinning them against the Bug river. Twenty Russian divisions were destroyed here. Nevertheless Russia's southern reserve armies concentrating round Kiev remained relatively strong and Hitler, always more interested in the Ukraine than Moscow, now made an important intervention. He halted the advance on Moscow and ordered Guderian to drive due south. Kleist was to strike north-east across the Dnieper and the two panzer group commanders were to meet 150 miles east of Kiev. And so they did, trapping fifty Russian divisions. The whole Ukraine passed under German occupation.

Greatly elated by this victory, Hitler ordered the advance on Moscow to be resumed. Guderian's place had been taken by Hoepner's group and it was a Hoth-Hoepner pincer that now cut out the centre of the Russian front, encircling forty-five divisions. So much for the first of the three defence lines round Moscow. The second was carried almost as easily. With Guderian now racing up from the south, the October situation maps at German headquarters appeared to show the envelopment of Moscow proceeding satisfactorily. But on the ground it was different. Torrential rain was gradually slowing down the movement of the panzers, supplies were failing to get through and the troops were almost fought out. The outstretched fingers which seemed to have Moscow in their grasp were just too weak to close.

Hitler's terrifying war machine had, for the moment at least, ground to a halt.

FINLAND

occupied
Norway

SWEDEN

Leningrad

front line 30 September

Moscow

USSR

occupied
Denmark

Smolensk

Ht

Hoepner

Minsk

Hp

Hoth

UNITED
KINGDOM

occupied
Holland

occupied
Belgium

NAZI GERMANY

Guderian

Poland

Kleist

G

K

EIRE

Bohemia-
Moravia

Slovakia

Kiev

Dnieper R.

Rostov

occupied France

SWISS

HUNGARY

Bug R.

UNOCCUPIED
(VICHY)
FRANCE

Banat

ROMANIA

Sebastopol

PORTUGAL

SPAIN

Croatia

Serbia

BULGARIA

TURKEY

Montenegro

ITALY

Albania

Gibraltar

Tangier

SPANISH

Ionian
Islands

occupied
Greece

Dodecanese
(ITALIAN)

Cyprus

Syria
(FREE
FRENCH)

FRENCH NORTH AFRICA
(VICHY)

Malta

Palestine

Trans-
Jordan

Key

Invasion of Russia, second phase

Ht Hoth

Hp Hoepner

G Guderian

K Kleist

BRITISH POSSESSIONS
AND PROTECTORATES

ITALIAN NORTH AFRICA

Rommel

Egypt

5 December
1941

WHEN IT BECAME APPARENT that the German drive on Moscow was fading out, Hitler's generals all advised him to withdraw and regroup. The Führer would have none of this: he wasn't going to give up an inch of conquered territory and, as far as he was concerned, anyone who suggested that he should was a coward or a traitor. One after another he sacked the commanders who refused to obey his stand-still order (Guderian and Hoepner were among the first to go); if the winter campaign demonstrated one thing, it was that Hitler was now in sole charge.

The campaign itself, though hailed at the time as a great Russian victory, fell well short of that. Stalin, sure that 1812 had come again, ordered an all-out, everywhere-at-once offensive that thrust alarming-looking salients into the German front. But the arms of the main Russian pincer movement, which were intended to meet near Smolensk, were held apart by the men of Hoepner's old panzer group, and the airborne forces that the Russians landed in a last effort to close the gap were nowhere near strong enough to do so. Similarly, the attempts to relieve Leningrad and Sebastopol both fell well short of their objectives. The one encirclement achieved, of seven German divisions at Demyansk, was laughed off by Hitler, who ordered the pocket to be supplied by air until it could be relieved in the spring. The encircling Russian forces proved unable to prevent either the supply or the relief.

So Hitler's New Order was to endure, if not for the thousand years he had in mind, at least for another year or two. As a political structure, what did it amount to? Germany, of course, was a lot bigger than before. Territories that had in the pre-war period belonged to Poland (the entire north-west of the country), France (Alsace-Lorraine), Yugoslavia (northern Slovenia) and Russia (Bialystok) were now German provinces. Then there was a roster of subject states ruled either by Nazi officials or Nazi

appointees: Bohemia-Moravia and Slovakia, Poland (what was left of it), Croatia and Serbia (carved out of Yugoslavia), and Ostland and the Ukraine (in the territories conquered from the USSR). Of somewhat similar standing were the countries under military occupation: Holland, Belgium, Denmark, Norway, Greece, the northern three-quarters of France and the Serbian part of Banat. Finally there were the sovereign states that had chosen to hitch their waggons to Hitler's star: Italy, Hungary, Bulgaria, Romania and Finland.

Most of this last group had been handsomely rewarded for their allegiance. Mussolini had got the bits of the Balkans he had always wanted: Dalmatia and the Ionian Islands, additions to his Albanian satrapy and Montenegro as a new one. The Hungarians had acquired nearly half the territory they had lost at the end of the First War; the Bulgars, everything they had lost then and the south of Yugoslavia as well. Gains by these two were made partly at Romania's expense and, what with the forced cession of Bessarabia and northern Bukovina to Russia in 1940, the Romanians had little enough to thank Hitler for initially. However, after the break with Russia, he gave them back Bessarabia and northern Bukovina and threw in a slice of the Ukraine (Transnistria) as well. As for the Finns, they were once again in possession of the territory they had lost in 1940.[1]

Events outside Europe need notice, especially as one of them was of critical importance. On 7 December 1941 the Japanese launched a surprise attack on the American Pacific Fleet at its anchorage in Pearl Harbor, Oahu Island, Hawaii. This precipitated the United States into what was now truly a world war because Hitler, when he heard of the attack, was so delighted that he decided to declare war on America himself. It was a gratuitous bit of folly. Maybe America was going to come in against him sooner or later, but why hasten the day? What conceivable advantage had he to gain, even of

the most temporary and tactical sort? There seems no answer except in terms of petulance and short-sightedness. But then maybe Hitler never did, never had, calculated the odds for more than the short term; maybe, indeed, that is why he had been so successful – in the short term.

1. Of the officially neutral states, two – unoccupied France (ruled by General Pétain from the provincial town of Vichy) and Franco's Spain – inclined to the Nazi side. Pétain could plead necessity for this; if it sometimes seemed that he pleaded it too often and too easily, most Frenchmen, at this stage in the war, gave him their support. Certainly the attempts of another French general, Charles de Gaulle, to persuade the overseas French to continue the struggle against the Germans met with very little response. The British hoped that he could at least bring Syria over to their side, but in the event they had to conquer it themselves; only after they had done so was de Gaulle able to install a 'Free French' governor. If this was disappointing for the British, the performance of Spain's General Franco was equally disappointing to the Germans: he wouldn't declare war on the British (he said Spain was too poor to afford another war) and he wouldn't even let the Germans take Gibraltar for him.

German air power and Rommel's Afrika Corps had between them badly shaken the British position in the Mediterranean, but they hadn't demolished it. Honours in the desert war between the Afrika Corps and the British Eighth Army were working out about even and if the British had their supply problems (they had to use the Cape route now), so did the Germans (British air and submarine forces made crossing the Mediterranean a hazardous and costly business).

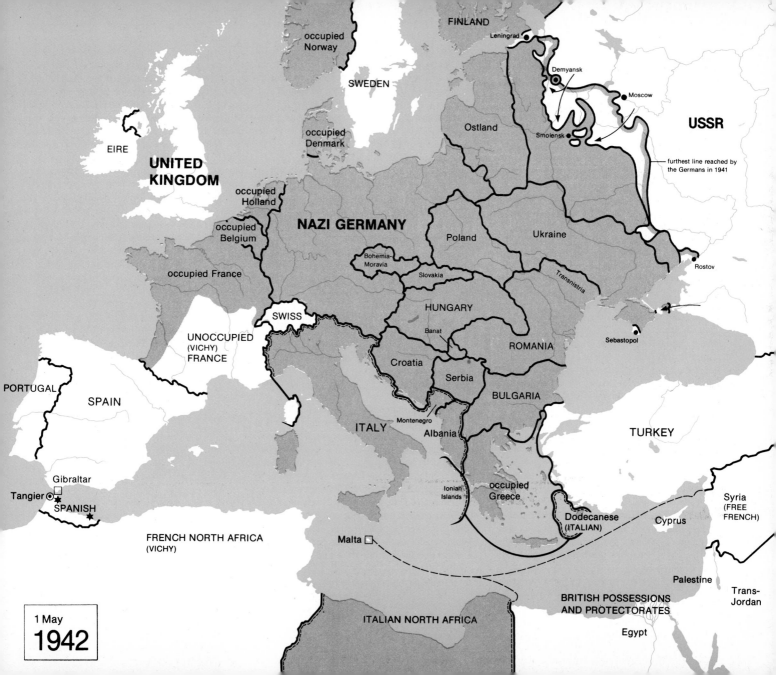

occupied Norway

FINLAND

Leningrad

SWEDEN

Demyansk

Moscow

occupied Denmark

Ostland

USSR

Smolensk

EIRE

UNITED KINGDOM

occupied Holland

NAZI GERMANY

furthest line reached by the Germans in 1941

occupied Belgium

Poland

Ukraine

occupied France

Bohemia-Moravia

Slovakia

Rostov

SWISS

HUNGARY

Transnistria

UNOCCUPIED (VICHY) FRANCE

Banat

PORTUGAL

SPAIN

Croatia

ROMANIA

Sebastopol

Serbia

BULGARIA

Montenegro

Gibraltar

ITALY

Albania

TURKEY

Tangier

SPANISH

Ionian Islands

occupied Greece

FRENCH NORTH AFRICA (VICHY)

Dodecanese (ITALIAN)

Cyprus

Syria (FREE FRENCH)

Malta

Palestine

Trans-Jordan

BRITISH POSSESSIONS AND PROTECTORATES

ITALIAN NORTH AFRICA

Egypt

1 May 1942

B Y APRIL 1942 Stalin had reluctantly conceded that the Germans were not going to be bundled out of Russia in a single campaign. What he didn't see was that it was now his turn to pull back. With the return of better weather the Germans recovered their mobility and re-established their tactical superiority. A series of local offensives lopped off the heads of the Russian salients; these protrusions, which had seemed so full of menace a few weeks earlier, now became death traps. Between the beginning of May and the end of June Soviet losses exceeded three-quarters of a million men; for anyone who thought that the German army had shot its bolt in 1941, it was a sobering curtain-raiser to the 1942 campaign.

This opened at the end of June with an economic rather than purely military objective. Hitler said that the German war machine needed more oil than the Romanian oilfields could supply; the only possible source was the Caucasus. The plan was to drive the Russians back to the line Voronezh-Stalingrad with one panzer army (Hoth's) and conquer the Caucasus with a second (Kleist's). It was a peculiar concept: where everyone was expecting a war-winning knockout blow, Hitler was limiting himself to underpinning Germany's economic position. Moreover, even if completely successful – and the campaign got off to a flawless start – it represented an increase in Germany's military commitment in Russia equivalent to the opening of a new front.

At the end of August the offensive was on schedule: German troops were at the gates of Stalingrad and only needed to take the city to complete their occupation of the Voronezh-Stalingrad line; Kleist's panzers were half-way to the Baku oilfield. September and October, however, were disappointing months. Stalingrad had to be fought for street by street and, as the Russians were able to send fresh formations across the Volga each night, the Germans were soon measuring their advances in

yards and counting their casualties in thousands. To expend in this sort of vicious First World War type attrition an army that had shown the world how to win by moving fast, and moving on, was stupid and unnecessary. Yet Hitler wouldn't give up: division followed division into the Stalingrad cauldron. Even so it proved impossible to take the entire city: the Russians clung on along the west bank of the Volga and the Germans couldn't get them out.

Kleist's advance in the Caucasus petered out at the same time. He could go no further unless the Führer released some of the panzer divisions in the Stalingrad area to his command. The German offensive had in fact stalled at the most dangerous phase in its development. There had never been enough German troops to man the vast extension of the front line; now the insatiable demands of the Stalingrad sector meant that only the most important points had any German troops at all. Between Voronezh and Stalingrad there were none, just a motley sequence of Italian, Hungarian and Romanian divisions. South of Stalingrad there were more Romanians. As the Russians were known to have moved south the armies they had been holding in reserve near Moscow, the situation looked not merely unsatisfactory, as Hitler thought, but ominous.

The Soviet counter-offensive began on 19/20 November. The pair of Romanian armies that were stationed on the flanks of the Germans in Stalingrad were simultaneously attacked by Russian mechanized units of great strength. Both crumbled so rapidly that the victorious Russian forces were able to join hands at Kalach on the Don three days later. They had encircled the twenty-two divisions – three of them armoured – of the German Sixth Army, a total of a quarter of a million men.

Whatever chance the Sixth Army had of breaking out, Hitler now threw away. Hoth was told to mount a counter-offensive and break back into Stalingrad; in the interim, the troops there were to stand fast and

he would arrange for them to be supplied by air. But the success at Demyansk in the preceding winter was not going to be easy to repeat. It was much harder to supply twenty-two divisions than seven and the Soviets were stronger both on land and in the air. Moreover, their strategic thinking had much improved. By 12 December when Hoth, using the only two panzer divisions available, launched his relief attack, the Russians had a new and larger set of pincers ready. On the 16th they launched an offensive on the upper Don which completely shattered the Italian army defending this sector. Then on the 24th they struck equally hard 300 miles away, against the Romanian army on Hoth's right flank. Faced with a second envelopment of the same proportions as Stalingrad, even Hitler saw the light. For the first time since the beginning of Operation Barbarossa, orders to pull back to defensible lines became permissible. As a result, both Hoth's and Kleist's armies made successful retreats.

Nothing could be done for the beleaguered men at Stalingrad. They fought on until 2 February, when the 90,000 survivors finally surrendered. Few of them lived to see the Fatherland again.

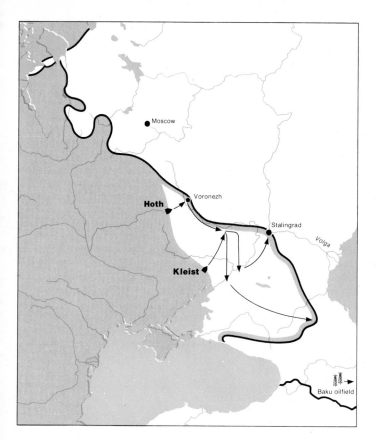

June to mid-November 1942
THE GERMAN ADVANCE

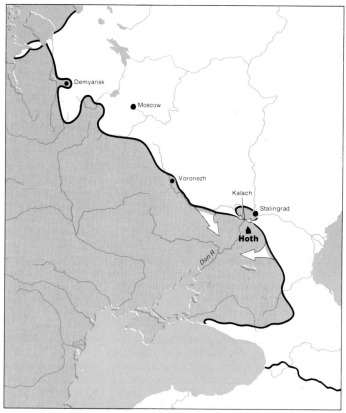

23 November to 25 December 1942
THE RUSSIAN COUNTER-ATTACK

THE RUSSIAN FRONT IN 1942

THE DISASTER AT STALINGRAD sobered Hitler considerably. He started listening to his generals again and even agreed to the evacuation of the Demyansk and Rzhev salients, until then regarded as triumphant examples of what willpower could do. This released enough troops to keep the northern and central fronts secure (though not enough to stop the Russians pushing along the southern shore of Lake Ladoga and relieving Leningrad); in the south, the German retreat continued till mid-February when Hoth, in a brilliantly timed counter-stroke, pinched off the Russians' lead tank division, drove its supporting forces back across the Donets and occupied the river's right bank. This put the front lines back where they had been a year earlier at the start of the Stalingrad campaign.

The German generals had shown they could tidy up a desperate-looking situation well enough; what would they come up with in the way of positive ideas for the 1943 summer season? The answer was a limited offensive to cut out the Kursk salient. General Model had charge of the seven panzer divisions that were to strike from the north; Hoth got the southern command and six panzer divisions. To the Russians, the only faintly reassuring aspect of this was that they knew pretty well what the Germans were planning; they fortified the flanks of the salient, built up their reserves and braced themselves for the blow. If they hadn't won a summer battle yet, at least this time they had their troops in the right place.

The German offensive began on 4 July. The panzers fought their way forward steadily for a week; then the attack began to lose impetus. Tank losses were very heavy; though the Russians' losses were even heavier, they, unlike the Germans, seemed to have the reserves to replace them. On the 12th Hitler called the offensive off. The panzers, he said, were required elsewhere; though there was some

truth in this he would hardly have cancelled a successful operation. The plain fact was that neither Model nor Hoth had achieved the breakthroughs expected of them.

The theatre for which Hitler needed troops was the Mediterranean, where things had been going badly for a long time. The last German success there had been Rommel's victory of June 1942, after which the Afrika Corps had chased the British half-way back to Suez. However, Rommel had failed to carry the Alamein position either then or in a second attempt three months later and in October the British struck back. The Afrika Corps was hit very hard in this battle and only just managed to extricate itself from Egypt; worse still, it couldn't stop to recuperate in Libya because the British and Americans now opened a new front in the western Mediterranean by landing in Morocco and Algeria (November), so Rommel had to pull back to Tunisia. He managed to hold out there through the winter because Hitler foolishly reinforced him, but in May 1943 the Afrika Corps (though not Rommel, who was in Europe) was finally forced to surrender.

Stalin was not impressed by this Anglo-American victory. There were 200 German divisions on Russian soil and what happened to the odd ten divisions deployed elsewhere – and ten divisions would be a generous estimate of the force Hitler committed to the African campaign – seemed hardly relevant. What he wanted to see was an Allied landing in France and the Germans forced to divide their army evenly between two major fronts. This was reasonable enough and the Americans didn't dispute it: it would be, in their view, the quickest way to win the war. The trouble was that as yet they didn't have sufficient troops to operate on this sort of scale and the British, who would have to provide most of the men, were very reluctant. Remembering the long casualty lists of the First World War, they proposed a smaller operation for 1943, the invasion of Italy. Only when the Americans were fully ready –

which would not be before mid-1944 – would they agree to a joint landing in France. Rather unhappily, the Americans agreed to go along with the British plan: on 10 July an Anglo-American army landed in Sicily.

Though Stalin had nothing but contempt for the British strategy, the Russians did get considerable benefit from the Sicilian invasion. On hearing of it Hitler not only stopped the Kursk offensive but ordered some of the divisions engaged in it to be transferred to Italy. More transfers were to follow, the troops being obtained by the evacuation of the salient north of Kursk. For Hitler, who hated ever pulling back, this was a remarkable turn-around and, one might think, something of an over-reaction. But he had his reasons. The Italians had had enough of the war and were planning to cop out. Fear of their Nazi partner had stopped them doing so before, but now that the Allies were on their doorstep this fear was no longer so compulsive: it should be possible, many Italians reasoned, to chuck Mussolini out and get the Allies in before Hitler could stop them. But no sooner had the Italians thought that than Hitler sensed it: when it came to a double-cross he had always been a hard man to beat.

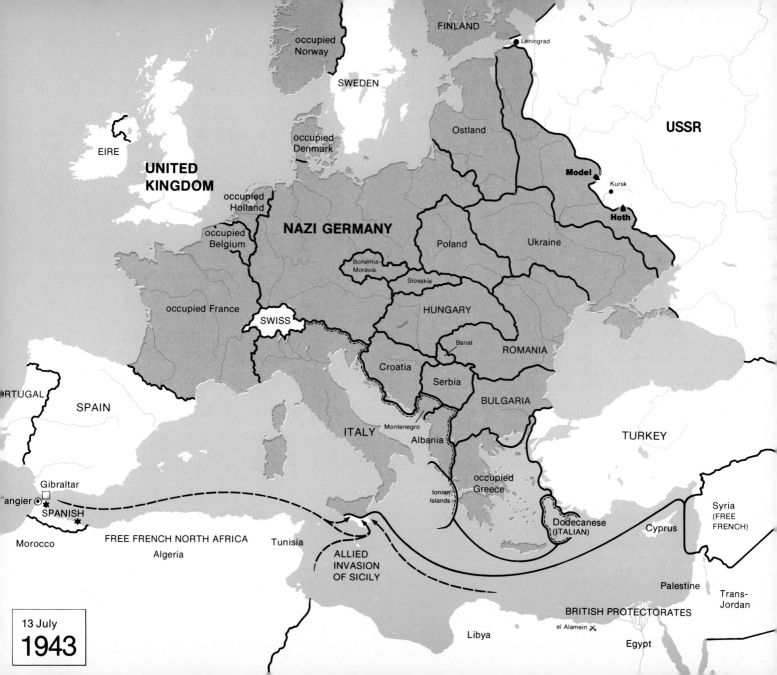

HITLER'S INTERVENTION in Italy was astonishingly successful. The Italians, playing it very warily, didn't announce their change of sides until the Allies had finished mopping up in Sicily and were actually landing on the Italian toe. The delay proved sufficient for Hitler to get a German army into the peninsula and form a defensive line across it. Hitler also managed to find out where the new Italian government had hidden Mussolini, rescue him and put him back in charge.[1]

Where Hitler didn't do so well – not by a long chalk – was in Russia. He had every reason to hope that the German forces there, for all that they had lost the strategic initiative, would be able to wage a successful defensive war. In fact things started to go wrong as soon as the Kursk offensive was called off. The Russians attacked all along the southern half of the front, forcing the German commanders to commit the few reserves they had at their disposal; a second wave of attacks found more gaps and this time there was no covering them: the Germans were forced back step by step from the Donets to the Dnieper. But at least it was still a relatively orderly retreat and had the advantage of bringing the German forces back to a shorter line; indeed the winter position of Army Group South was much the same as the one the High Command had wanted it to take up in the first place.

Unfortunately Army Group South proved no more capable of holding the Dnieper than the Donets. Stalin was determined to get the Germans out of the Ukraine and was prepared to commit every man and gun he could muster to achieve this object. Throughout the winter he launched one division after another across the Dnieper, hammering to pieces each successive German position; by the spring of 1944 the leading units of the Red Army were through the Ukraine and advancing into Poland and Romania.

The only disappointing aspect of the Red Army's performance in this victorious campaign was its failure to grip and destroy any sizeable German force. For this, Stalin's strategy of attacking all along the line was certainly to blame. It might have got Army Group South on the run, but it also meant that none of the envelopments achieved was strong enough to hold: time and again apparently doomed German forces proved able to fight their way out of encirclement and get back to safety. Soviet plans for the summer of 1944 show that this point had not gone unnoticed: the next pincer movement was to be both simple and strong.

The Red Army had already defeated both Army Group South and Army Group North (driven back from Leningrad in January); now it was the turn of Army Group Centre. The battle began on 22 June, the third anniversary of Hitler's invasion of Russia. Initially the Soviet attacks focused on Vitebsk and Bobruisk, two towns 150 miles apart that Hitler had declared special strong points and, if anything, over-garrisoned. Within five days both had been cut out of the German line and Russian tank forces were streaming past them in a converging attack on Minsk. The arms of this pincer, which closed on 4 July, proved amply strong enough to keep and crush what they held. And it was a staggering haul. Army Group Centre, desperately trying to re-form along the old Polish frontier, found that it had only twelve of its forty divisions left.

Hitler barely had time to think about the gaping hole torn in his eastern front: he was trying to stave off an equal disaster in the west. The British and Americans had finally landed in France on 6 June; though they had needed time to build up the forces in their Normandy bridgehead to full strength, they were ready to try for a break-out by the beginning of July. This they achieved – at least the Americans did – at the end of July. Swinging round from the eastern end of the bridgehead, the Americans tried to pin the Germans back against the British; though they weren't quite quick enough to catch the panzer divisions they were after, they did destroy the German position in France. Hitler lost at least as heavily as he had in central Russia.[2]

As the Nazi forces streamed back towards the Fatherland it looked as if 1944 would see the end of the Third Reich. But the closer the Allied forces got to the German frontier the shorter they became of supplies and the fewer the troops they could keep in action. Finally the Germans discovered that the forces pursuing them had become too weak to press home their attacks and a front line formed again. At most points the Allies were still well short of the Rhine; nowhere were they across it.[3]

1. Hitler punished the Italians for their defection by moving Germany's frontier south, to roughly where Austria's had been in 1914, and giving Dalmatia to the puppet Croats, who had turned out to be nasty enough to satisfy even him.
2. The Allied (almost exclusively American) landing in the south of France wasn't the sort of strategic pincer movement it looks like on the map but just a way of transferring troops from the Mediterranean theatre to the main front. Italy was turning out to be exactly the strategic cul-de-sac that the Americans had always said it would and they wanted to reduce their commitment there as quickly as possible.
3. Much the same thing happened in the east, where the Russian advance stalled in the eastern suburbs of Warsaw. Tragically, the Polish Resistance misread the situation and, thinking liberation by the Russians was only a few days away, staged a rising in Warsaw proper, west of the Vistula. Their aim was not merely to give the retreating Nazis a suitably punishing send-off but to get the flag of independent Poland aloft before the Russians arrived and imposed a puppet communist government on them. Hopelessly under-equipped for the task they had set themselves, they were cut to bits by the Germans over the next eight weeks.

FINLAND

occupied
Norway

SWEDEN

Leningrad

Ostland

Vitebsk

USSR

occupied
Denmark

Minsk

Bobruisk

Donets R

EIRE

UNITED
KINGDOM

occupied
Holland

NAZI GERMANY

Warsaw

Dnieper R

ALLIED FORCES IN FRANCE

occupied
Belgium

Poland

Bohemia-
Moravia

Slovakia

occupied France

SWISS

HUNGARY

Fascist Italy

Banat

ORTUGAL

SPAIN

Croatia

ROMANIA

Serbia

ALLIED FORCES
IN THE
MEDITERRANEAN

Montenegro

Albania

BULGARIA

TURKEY

Gibraltar

Tangier

SPANISH

occupied
Greece

Cyprus

Syria
(FREE
FRENCH)

FREE FRENCH NORTH AFRICA

Malta

BRITISH PROTECTORATES

Palestine

Trans-
Jordan

Libya

Egypt

20 August
1944

Key

front line 4 July

front line 20 August

ALTHOUGH by the late summer of 1944 the Allies' direct thrusts at Germany were temporarily running out of steam, it was clear to anyone but the most fanatical Nazi that Hitler had lost the war. Finland, Romania, Hungary and Bulgaria all had peace feelers out and the Romanians may well have reached an understanding with the Russians before the Red Army began its 20 August offensive against them.[1] Certainly the Romanian soldiers threw their guns away as soon as the Russians attacked, leaving the twenty or so German divisions in the country to stand on their own – and be quickly overwhelmed. By the end of the month both Romania and Bulgaria were out of the war; by the beginning of the next both were back in again on the Russian side. September also saw the Russians unleash a massive offensive against Army Group North, which made up the Finns' minds for them: they accepted Stalin's terms (the 1940 frontier in the south, but a line much more in Russia's favour in the north and a very heavy reparations bill) and left the war. Effectively, Army Group North did too: by October it had been penned into the Kurland peninsula.

The loss of Romania and Bulgaria meant – as even Hitler could see – the evacuation of Greece, Albania and southern Yugoslavia. This operation was carried out successfully, as was a coup in Budapest which brought the Hungarians back into line. By November Hitler had established a defensive perimeter across the western Balkans, which held reasonably well, partly because the Russian force invading Hungary had to subject Budapest to a formal siege (the city didn't fall till February 1945).

The German army's losses in 1944 were immense, adding up to the equivalent of more than 100 divisions. Nevertheless, during this period Hitler managed to scrape up a reserve of twenty-five divisions, which he committed in December to a replay of his 1940 triumph in France, an offensive in the Ardennes. General Model was given charge of the operation. He planned it well: when the attack went in – against the Americans, on 16 December – it was a complete surprise. As the panzers raced for the Meuse and the Allies desperately searched for the troops they needed to rebuild their line, the world wondered if Hitler had managed to bring it off again. But the Allies had the men and Hitler didn't; the tide of battle soon turned and by January the Allies had resumed their advance. The British, Americans and French gradually forced their way forward to the Rhine; the Russians burst across the Vistula and then, after clearing Pomerania and Silesia, reached the Oder-Neisse line.

It was now mid-March. For the last two months Hitler had been directing operations from a bomb-proof bunker deep beneath the Chancellery in Berlin. His orders were always the same: stand fast, hold on, shoot any waverers and sell your own lives as dearly as possible. But the military situation was now quite beyond control: the Rhine front collapsed as soon as the Allies challenged it and, leaving the last German army in the west locked up in the Ruhr, the British and Americans swept forward to the Elbe. The Russians didn't move till a month later; then, on 16 April, after a massive bombardment of the far bank, they crossed the Oder. Within a week they were on the outskirts of Berlin.

Hitler decided to stay where he was. He held his mid-day conferences as usual, charting the progress of the Russians across the city block by block. He also composed his political testament. He denounced his oldest friends – they were traitors all of them; he repudiated the German people – they had proved unworthy of him; he railed against the Jewish conspiracy that he believed had brought him down. Then he simultaneously clenched his teeth on a cyanide capsule and shot himself through the temple.

Over the next week the German armies still in the field surrendered to the Allied forces encircling them: the war in Europe, which had cost some thirty million lives, was finally over.[2]

1. The initial spearheads are shown on the previous map.
2. About twenty million of the dead were Russians. Rather more of them were civilians than Red Army men and the vast majority died far from any battlefield. Starvation, slave-labour conditions, terror and counter-terror, all played their part, with Stalin probably responsible for nearly as many deaths as Hitler. Where the Nazis were clear leaders was in the maltreatment of prisoners-of-war (probably only one million of the six million Russian soldiers they captured survived the war) and the elimination of specific ethnic groups (they murdered five million Jews, nearly all of them in Poland or Russia).
In the Far East the fighting went on until August when the Americans made the nuclear strikes on Hiroshima (6 August) and Nagasaki (9 August). This forced the Japanese to face up to the fact that the war was irretrievably lost and they surrendered within the week.

1 January 1945

Mid-March to mid-April 1945

NAZI GERMANY IN 1945

WHATEVER ELSE there is to be said about the Second World War, it had, in terms of Europe's political geography, a very simple outcome: Germany lost and Russia won. The Germans paid for their defeat in two ways: they lost everything east of the Oder-Neisse line (most of it to Poland, but the northern half of East Prussia to the USSR), while what was left of the country was split into two halves, West Germany (the 'Federal Republic') and East Germany (the 'Democratic Republic'). West Germany, a parliamentary democracy set up in 1949 in the area occupied by the Americans, British and French, has since become the economic leader of the West European community. East Germany, which developed out of the Red Army's occupation zone, hasn't developed into anything much: it remains a Soviet satellite of the most restricted and restrictive sort.[1]

Soviet client states feature largely in the new Europe; indeed if Germany lost in two ways, Russia gained in two, direct and via satellite. The direct gains include everything occupied during the 1939–41 honeymoon with Hitler (bar the province of Bialystok, which was retroceded to Poland) plus the northern half of East Prussia and the tail end of pre-war Czechoslovakia. It sounds a lot, but the present-day Soviet frontier is more often behind than in front of the Tsarist one and, of the two genuinely new acquisitions, East Prussia was reasonably conceded to the Russians as a bit of rough justice as was Ruthenia (previously Czechoslovakian) on ethnic grounds. The Russo-Polish frontier is conspicuously fair, being near enough the same as the one proposed by the British at the end of the First World War. Well might Stalin claim that, considering Russia's past sufferings and present strength, his territorial demands were mainly remarkable for their modesty.

What makes a mockery of any such claim is, of course, the way the Soviet dictator imposed the instruments of his will on every country within his reach – which amounted to every country unfortunate enough to be 'liberated' by the Red Army. Only the Finns were allowed to retain their independence; the Poles, Czechs, Hungarians, Romanians and Bulgars were all forced to accept communist administrations entirely subservient to the Russian interest. This both alienated and alarmed the western democracies and, under American leadership, they formed an opposing bloc. What had been greeted as peace quickly changed into an era of 'Cold War'. And so it has continued for the last thirty years. Stalin's successors have tried hard to appear less cold-blooded than he, but under pressure – as when the Hungarians tried to leave the Soviet camp in 1956 or, twelve years later, when the Czechs sought to liberalize their regime – they have reacted every bit as ruthlessly. The ideological gulf remains unbridged: there has been *détente* but no *rapprochement*.

Whether this situation is comfortable or not, it is certainly stable. The frontiers agreed in the immediate post-war years have remained unchanged ever since, a matter of more than thirty years. When one considers that frontiers in the western half of the continent are actually the same as they were before the war and that in the south-east they are almost the same (the Yugoslavs got Istria and Zara at the war's end, the Greeks got the Dodecanese and the Bulgars were allowed to retain the southern Dobruja), it is arguable that what we are looking at is the end result of a maturing process that has finally given Europe the frontiers it needs. There is probably something to this – but there is probably as much in the idea that Stalin solved the problems that had been troubling pre-war Europe by drastic surgery. As was his wont, he drew a new map and fitted the people to it: he cleared Russia of Poles and Poland (and Czechoslovakia) of Germans.

Whatever the reason, it does seem that Europe has settled down in a way that some other parts of the world have not. This is apparent from a glance at the areas that get marginal treatment in this *Atlas*: North Africa and nearer Asia. While Europe has, in terms of political geography, stood still for thirty years, these lands have been transformed. For a start they have been decolonized, the middle-eastern countries in the immediate post-war years (Syria, the Lebanon and Trans-Jordan in 1946, Egypt in 1947 and Palestine in 1948), the rest of the North African countries bar Algeria in the 1950s (Libya in 1951, Tunisia and Morocco in 1956) and Algeria, where the whole process was delayed by the attempt of the million-strong white settlers to preserve their special status, in 1962. Moreover, though in every case but one decolonization has simply transformed a colonial territory into an independent state, the exception has created such tension throughout the area that it seems likely there is a lot more history of a very old-fashioned sort still to come. The state of Israel, proclaimed by the Jewish settlers in Palestine when the British left the country, has won all four of the wars it has fought with its Arab neighbours – in 1948, in 1956, in 1967 and 1973 – and currently its army is in control of all the Arab bits of Palestine and slices of Syria and Egypt too. But few believe that the last word has yet been said on Israel's frontiers or indeed on the final shape of the states to the north and east of it: Lebanon, Syria and Jordan (as Trans-Jordan has been known since 1949).[2]

Historical atlases don't usually deal in geographical change, but there are clearly a lot more lakes in Russia on this last map than there were when we started. Soviet engineers are responsible: in their quest for more and more hydro-electric power, they have built a great many dams; these new lakes are reservoirs created by the half-dozen largest of them. In every case the blueprints for these projects were drawn up in Stalin's day and three of them had

(continued overleaf)

NORWAY

FINLAND

SWEDEN

DENMARK

EIRE

UNITED
KINGDOM

HOLLAND

West
Berlin

EAST
GERMANY

POLAND

USSR

BELGIUM

WEST
GERMANY

CZECHOSLOVAKIA

FRANCE

SWISS

AUSTRIA

HUNGARY

ROMANIA

YUGOSLAVIA

BULGARIA

PORTUGAL

SPAIN

ITALY

ALBANIA

GREECE

TURKEY

Gibraltar
(BRITISH)

Ceuta
(SPANISH)

Melilla
(SPANISH)

MOROCCO

ALGERIA

MALTA

CYPRUS
Turkish

Greek

Akrotiri and
Dhekelia
(BRITISH)

SYRIA

LEBANON

ISRAEL

JORDAN

TUNISIA

LIBYA

EGYPT

1 January
1980

Key

Areas under
Israeli military
occupation

been completed before his death: the Ivankovo reservoir, finished in 1937 and visible to the north-east of Moscow in the conurbation map for that date, the far bigger Rybinsk reservoir due north of Moscow, which was filled in 1941 and so makes its first appearance on the map that shows Hitler's panzers scissoring their way into Russia, and the post-war Tsimlyansk reservoir, which together with the Volga-Don Canal was completed in 1952. Indeed, the whole sequence is a fitting memorial to the Soviet dictator who changed things most people think of as too big to change, whose merciless energy created a whole new range of demographic, political and economic facts.

1. All the occupying powers got a slice of Berlin. The Russian sector became the capital of East Germany, while the American, British and French sectors became West Berlin, an enclave of West German territory within East Germany.

2. The British have almost, but not quite, withdrawn from the Mediterranean, their only remaining bases being Gibraltar and the two airfield complexes they retained on Cyprus when they gave the island its independence in 1960. They left Malta in 1964.

The Greek majority on Cyprus tried to make the island part of Greece in 1974, but a Turkish invasion put a stop to that; it also created a state of *de facto* partition that looks like becoming permanent.

INDEX

This is an index to the text only. Place names mentioned in the text are usually to be found on the accompanying map; in the case of multiple entries, this is most likely to be true of the first entry.

Penguin Books Ltd, Harmondsworth, Middlesex, England
Penguin Books, 40 West 23rd Street, New York, New York 10010, U.S.A.
Penguin Books Australia Ltd, Ringwood, Victoria, Australia
Penguin Books Canada Ltd, 2801 John Street, Markham, Ontario, Canada L3R 1B4
Penguin Books (N.Z.) Ltd, 182–190 Wairau Road, Auckland 10, New Zealand

First published in 1982
Reprinted 1984

Made and printed in Great Britain by
Butler & Tanner Ltd, Frome, Somerset
Set in Monophoto Times
by Southern Positives and Negatives (SPAN), Lingfield, Surrey